TOUCHDOWN TONY

RUNNING WITH A PURPOSE

TONY NATHAN

HOWARD BOOKS
AN IMPRINT OF SIMON & SCHUSTER, INC.

New York   Nashville   London   Toronto   Sydney   New Delhi

Howard Books
An Imprint of Simon & Schuster, Inc.
1230 Avenue of the Americas
New York, NY 10020

First Howard Books hardcover edition September 2015

HOWARD and colophon are trademarks of Simon & Schuster, Inc.

For information about special discounts for bulk purchases,
please contact Simon & Schuster Special Sales
at 1-866-506-1949 or business@simonandschuster.com.

The Simon & Schuster Speakers Bureau can bring authors
to your live event. For more information or to book an event,
contact the Simon & Schuster Speakers Bureau
at 1-866-248-3049 or visit our website at www.simonspeakers.com.

Interior design by Akasha Archer

Manufactured in the United States of America

3   5   7   9   10   8   6   4   2

Library of Congress Cataloging-in-Publication Data

Nathan, Tony, 1956–
Touchdown Tony / Tony Nathan.—First Edition.
pages cm
ISBN 978-1-5011-1851-7 (hc)—ISBN (invalid) 978-1-5011-2573-7 (tp)—
ISBN 978-1-5011-1853-1 (ebook)   1. Nathan, Tony, 1956–
2. Football players—Alabama—Biography.   3. Miami Dolphins
(Football team)—History.   4. Football coaches—United States—
Biography.   I. Title.
GV939.N36A3 2015
796.332092—dc23
[B]   2015016728

ISBN 978-1-5011-1851-7
ISBN 978-1-5011-1853-1 (ebook)

CONTENTS

CONTENTS

FOREWORD
Tony Dungy

I have known Tony Nathan for more than thirty years. I coached against him when he was a running back for the NFL's Miami Dolphins, and then he worked with me as an assistant coach on my staff with the Tampa Bay Buccaneers from 1996 to 2001.

I thought I knew him quite well, but I have to admit that I didn't know much about Tony's early life until I read this book. He's a very humble man and doesn't talk about his own achievements very much. But after reading about what Tony initially endured and then accomplished at Woodlawn High School in Birmingham, Alabama, during the early 1970s, I have to say that I'm not surprised. I know the kind of man Tony is, and I witnessed his courage, determination, and humility when he was a player and an assistant coach.

The Bible makes it clear that God has a purpose for each of our lives, and there's no doubt in my mind that God put Tony at Woodlawn High School for a very specific reason—a purpose that went far beyond winning football games. I believe God used Tony to help bring a football team, a high school, and a community closer together during a time of great turmoil. Tony was a humble and reluctant superstar, but his courage and willingness to accept the challenge speaks volumes about the type of man he was then and is today.

Like Tony, I grew up during the Civil Rights Movement of the 1960s and 1970s. However, while I was raised in Jackson, Michigan, Tony grew up at ground zero of the struggle in Birmingham.

Like Tony's remarkable parents, my mother and father taught me to look past the color of a person's skin and to turn my head to the racism and prejudice we faced at the time. It wasn't always an easy thing to do, but my parents taught me that intelligence, poise, leadership, humility, respect, and dignity were the characteristics that would make me successful in life. Those were the same lessons that Louise and William Nathan taught to Tony and his brothers and sisters. And those lessons served him well.

After becoming a star at Woodlawn High School and then

the University of Alabama, Tony played on several great teams during his NFL career with the Miami Dolphins. While Dolphins quarterback Dan Marino and wide receivers Mark Clayton and Mark Duper were probably the best-known players on his teams, Tony was always the guy we were concerned with stopping because he had the ability to hurt you in so many ways.

While I was the defensive coordinator for the Pittsburgh Steelers, I had to devise ways to contain Tony, which was never easy. He could hurt you as a runner, receiver, blocker, or kick returner. He might not have been the most recognizable Dolphin to the fans, but as an opposing coach I knew what a vital role he played in the team's success.

One of the things that impressed me most about Tony as a player was that he was always evolving. In high school, he was rarely asked to block and seldom caught the ball out of the backfield. At Alabama, however, he became a punishing blocker in Coach Paul "Bear" Bryant's wishbone offense. His willingness to sacrifice his personal statistics and to block for his teammates was one of the reasons he was one of Coach Bryant's favorite players. He was unselfish and did his job when he wasn't running the ball. Tony was willing to do whatever he needed to do to help his team win. Tony didn't catch many balls at Alabama, but he became a potent threat as a receiver in the NFL through hard work and practice.

His willingness to evolve and to learn all aspects of the game made him a great coach after he retired as a player. When Tony joined my coaching staff with the Buccaneers, the franchise had endured thirteen consecutive losing seasons. In many of those seasons, the Buccaneers were among the worst teams in the league. There was no tradition of winning and no standard of excellence. The Buccaneers went 6–10 in our first season with the team in 1996 as we struggled to develop an identity and a winning attitude. That year, Tony was a calming influence and a tremendous role model for our entire team, but especially for our rookie fullback Mike Alstott.

The following year we drafted another running back, Florida State All-American Warrick Dunn. Our running game immediately blossomed and the Buccaneers finished 10–6, making the playoffs for the first time in fifteen years. Mike and Warrick, under Tony's direction, were both selected for the Pro Bowl.

Our teams reached the playoffs four times during our six seasons together, and I think we really helped change the way the Buccaneers were regarded, not only in the Tampa area, but also throughout the National Football League. The year after we left Tampa, the Buccaneers reached the Super Bowl under coach Jon Gruden, and there is no doubt in my mind that Tony and my other assistant coaches helped lay the foundation for over a decade of football excellence in Tampa.

As an assistant coach, Tony was a lot like me—we didn't like to raise our voices or scream at our players. I think it's a trait we learned from our fathers. When I was trying to become a head coach in the NFL, a few owners and general managers told me I wouldn't be forceful enough or tough enough to oversee a team. I guess they didn't think I could strike enough fear into my players, which they believed was one of the requirements to be a successful NFL head coach.

What those team owners and general managers didn't know is that if you have the right message, the players will hear your voice. You have to find creative ways to get your point across, but you don't have to change your personality. I think Tony stayed true to his character while coaching and getting the most out of his players.

My first head coach, Chuck Noll, won four Super Bowl championships with the Pittsburgh Steelers. When I joined his staff as a young assistant coach, he told me that a coach's job was simply to help each one of his players be the best that they could be, on and off the field. In my opinion, Tony Nathan epitomized that idea. He always made those around him better, and he helped his players grow as men. By Coach Noll's definition, Tony was not only a great player and a great coach, but a great man as well. Since Tony's early days at Woodlawn High School, his motivation has been to make a difference in others' lives. It's one of the reasons he continues to shine today.

TOUCHDOWN TONY

CHAPTER ONE

MOM AND POPS

As a twelve-year-old kid in 1968, I had no notions of being a professional football player. In fact, I hadn't played much football up until that point. Sure, I'd played with the other boys in my neighborhood, but I'd never played on an actual team in an organized league. While I enjoyed playing the sport, I didn't really like running with the football. I much preferred being the one who did the tackling, rather than being the one who was getting tackled.

Even though I didn't have big dreams for my future, I knew two things I *didn't* want to do when I became an adult: I didn't want to pick cotton, and I didn't want to work in a steel mill. My father, William Nathan II, worked the graveyard shift at Conner Steel, which was one of the bigger plants in Birmingham, Alabama. My father, whom my family calls Pops, started his career as a laborer in the steel mill. Because of his strong work ethic, he was eventually promoted to mechanic. Pops went to school and learned how to fix things—a skill that was very valuable at the steel mill. My father worked hard, and I rarely heard him complain about his job. But working at the steel mill was dangerous, and hearing the horror stories about the accidents there made me realize that I wanted no part of it. Pouring steel wasn't easy, and the plant was always hot——especially during the sweltering Alabama summers. I remember seeing my dad covered in grease, dirt, and sweat when he came home in the morning. He always looked exhausted. I was sure that I didn't want to punch the clock at the mill when I was older.

I also knew I didn't want to pick cotton, because that's what I did when I spent time at my grandfather's farm. My paternal grandfather, William Nathan, had a farm near Uniontown, Alabama, which is where my dad grew up. My grandfather's farm was about ten acres, and he raised cows and other animals. He also planted cotton, corn, watermelons, peanuts, potatoes, and other fruits and vegetables every spring. Farming was hard work, and my grandfather went to the fields every day. When I was twelve or thirteen, I spent a lot of weekends and most of the summer working my grandfather's farm. He woke up every morning about 4:00 a.m., and then he'd get me up a couple of hours later. Though I could have helped him with his earliest chores, he'd always let me sleep a little longer. We'd harness a mule to a wagon, and then the mule would take us out to his land, which was a couple of miles from the house. The mule knew exactly where to go, so we'd sleep during the short ride.

Once we were old enough, my two brothers, two sisters (my biological aunt Erma Gean was only a couple of years older than me, so I refer to her as my sister), and I picked cotton, hoed weeds, and helped my grandfather harvest the fruits and vegetables. During those weekends and hot summer days, we usually worked from sunup till sundown. Those days were *long*. The constant threat of being eaten alive by fire ants and gnats made it even worse. It was difficult work, and I didn't want to do it, but I learned to respect anyone who did. It was a tough way to make a living. More than anything, it taught me what I didn't want to do with the rest of my life. Don't get me wrong: I appreciated what my father and grandfather did for a living, and I certainly didn't think the work was beneath me.

By having me work on the farm, my dad and grandfather

gave me an opportunity to see how they were raised and what they had to do to survive, and I've always respected them for what they did. And they definitely passed on a strong work ethic to me—a valuable lesson that has served me well.

Even though I didn't want any cotton picking in my future, I also knew that if farming was what I had to do to make my way in life, then that's what I would do. In the fields, I learned that you do what you have to do to make ends meet and provide for your family. And if I had to work in a steel mill, then I knew I could do that, too. If it was good enough for my father, it was good enough for me. My father was my mentor and is now my best friend. I can't thank him enough for providing me with the chance to do what I wanted in life.

Pops didn't have much in terms of material possessions when he was growing up. He went to school, and he worked on the farm; he did what he needed to do to help his family survive. After high school, my dad joined the army and was stationed at Fort Rucker in Dale County, Alabama. A week before my dad was to be deployed to fight in the Korean War, the United States and North Korea signed an armistice ending the three-year-old conflict. Obviously, he was among the lucky ones. Pops spent the next two years working as a drill sergeant at Fort Benning in Columbus, Georgia. He was discharged from the army in July 1955, following the end of the Korean War.

The year before my dad joined the army in 1953, he met my mother, Louise, whose sister was dating one of his brothers. My mom said she really wasn't attracted to my dad initially, but he seemed to grow on her because he was at her house so often. Even though my mom was only fifteen years old, Pops persuaded her parents to let them marry on Christmas Day 1955. My dad was twenty-two years old on his wedding day. While my mother would be considered too young nowadays, they've been happily married for nearly sixty years. They taught me a lot about the sacrifices a husband and wife have to make for a marriage to work.

....

Pops didn't have much in terms of material
possessions when he was growing up, but he did
what he needed to do to help his family survive.

....

In the spring of 1955, Pops moved to Birmingham and my mom joined him there the next spring, where they started their lives together. I was born on December 14, 1956. My sister, Diane, was born two years later, and then my brothers, Vincent and Cedric, came along after her. I was five years older than Vince and ten years older than Cedric, and I still regret that I missed so much of Cedric's childhood. I was out of the house by the time he went to high school, but despite our age difference, we're still very close today.

When I was seven years old, my aunt Erma Gean came to live with us in Birmingham after my maternal grandmother died. Erma Gean was only two years older than I was, so she's always been more like my sister than my aunt. When I was a kid, she and I spent some fun times together at my maternal grandparents' farm. My mom's parents, Dorsey and Mary Williams, lived about twenty-five miles from Grandpa Nathan's farm. I loved spending time with Erma Gean. She and I liked to run through the cotton rows and cornfields together. We ran to the end of dirt roads and back. She was probably the one who taught me how to run. Erma Gean was bigger than me, and I had a difficult time keeping up with her. Even though she might have been faster than me, I was determined to ramp up my speed. By the end of the day, my calves were usually swollen from trying to catch her. Sometimes, we rode my grandfather's big pig in the front yard, which was quite an adventure. Erma Gean and I were always looking for ways to have fun.

Once I reached high school and was old enough to drive, I went to work for a man who owned a farm near my aunt Elizabeth's house. The man paid me three dollars a day to drive a tractor. I was lucky that I didn't have to help bale the hay, like the other boys who were younger than me. They would load up a wagon with hay, and then I'd drive the tractor to the barn. At the time, three dollars a day was a lot of money to me, so at the end of the summer, I didn't want to go back to Birmingham. But Pops told the farmer he couldn't keep me because I had to go back to school. Being young and naive, I tried to talk my dad into letting me stay. I told him I'd just drop out of school. Fortunately, Pops persuaded me to go back to Birmingham by promising me a weekly allowance of three dollars. That's all it took to change my mind.

My mother and father couldn't have been more different, and you know what they say about how opposites attract. That was my parents in a nutshell. My father is a soft-spoken man and always has a smile on his face. People like to say that Pops has never met a stranger. I have great admiration for my father regarding the way he treats other people and shows them respect. He's a levelheaded man and rarely becomes angry—I remember only a very few times when he actually raised his voice. My father is a cool individual.

My dad's friends called him "Coon Man" because he's a great coon hunter. Hunting has always been his outlet; it's how he gets away from everybody else and the chaos of life. He loves being in the woods, and while he was still working in the noisy, busy steel mill, he enjoyed the freedom of the woods and having time to relax. He also likes to train dogs to chase coons, so while I was growing up, we usually had a backyard full of hunting dogs. As soon as the school day ended on Friday, we'd jump into my dad's truck and head to my grandfather's farm.

I liked going to the farm with Pops, but I didn't like to hunt. In fact, I've only been hunting with him twice. The first time, my mom made Pops take me because she wasn't convinced he was actually hunting when he left home. After Pops came home empty-handed two or three times, my mother started to wonder if he wasn't really spending the weekend at a honky-tonk. My dad blamed it on his sorry dogs. Still, my mom made him take me the next time for good luck. My grandfather came along, too, but we didn't see a coon the entire weekend. At the end of Saturday night's hunt, I told him, "Pops, now we're in trouble. Momma sent me with you for good luck."

....

After Pops returned from hunting empty-handed two or three times, my mother started to wonder if he wasn't really spending the weekend at a honky-tonk.

....

Fortunately, my grandfather had a raccoon in his deep freezer that he'd recently killed. We stopped by to get it, then let it thaw out on the way home. When we showed it to my mom, she said, "I'm going to have to send Tony with you every time!"

That wasn't exactly what I wanted to hear. Although I enjoyed spending time with my dad and grandfather, I wasn't particularly excited about hunting. You have to hunt coons at night, and you never know whether you'll actually see one. It was usually pretty cold when we hunted, and there wasn't enough action to keep me interested—or warm. I would have rather been playing baseball, basketball, or football with my friends than chasing a raccoon through the woods. I guess I don't have the patience required for hunting.

On our second hunting trip, I followed Pops around for what seemed like forever. His dogs finally picked up a raccoon's scent and took off running. We started to chase the dogs, but I quickly lost sight of my dad, who was in front of me. His dogs chased the raccoon up a tree. Pops could hear the dogs, but he couldn't find me. After going in circles for about thirty minutes, his dogs lost interest in the coon and came back. Then they started barking and charged another tree. Pops found me leaning against a tree, sound asleep.

"Hey, Pops, where's the truck?" I asked, after he woke me up.

"I gotta go shoot this coon," he said. "You go back to the truck."

When Pops returned to the truck, I said, "You're going to have to get you another partner. This is the last hunt for me."

I never went hunting with Pops again. Pops loves the sport,

and it works for him—but it isn't for me. Spending all night in the woods just isn't my idea of fun. My brothers, Vince and Cedric, didn't like coon hunting much, either. Fortunately, Pops found a boy in our neighborhood who liked to hunt, and they've been hunting together for about thirty-five years.

While Pops is a quiet man, my mother is loud, boisterous, and outspoken. When Mom came to watch my games, she was usually the loudest person in the stands. If the woman has an opinion, she'll let you know what it is. She is spunky and likes to get her point across. When my mom wants to talk, she doesn't mind talking. When she's tired of talking about something, she'll let you know that, too.

My mother was a homemaker, and her primary job was raising her family. She taught herself how to sew and earned extra money by making clothes for others. To save money, she made clothes for my brothers, sisters, and me. My clothes didn't have tags from department stores, but I knew no one else could buy replicas of them—my clothes were one of a kind. My mom also worked as a caretaker and tended to the sick and elderly when she was needed. She was always busy and rarely sat still.

Make no mistake: my mom was the boss when I was growing up. She had to raise three boys and two girls. She had her hands full. She is a big-boned woman with a large frame and booming voice. She didn't play around when it came to discipline, and she didn't mind if others disciplined us, too. Where I grew up, the parents believed it took a village to raise a child. If you were at a friend's house and stepped out of line, his parents took it upon themselves to discipline and spank you. When we returned home, our parents spanked us again because somebody else had to discipline us. The threat of double jeopardy usually kept us out of trouble.

....

> Where I grew up, the parents believed
> it took a village to raise a child.

....

My momma made it very clear to us that we did not want to embarrass our family. We were taught to respect other people, obey our elders, and not get into trouble. She didn't want us bringing negative attention to our family. My momma likes to say that she and my dad tried to raise us to do right and then let God do the rest. As Proverbs 22:6 teaches, "Start children off on the way they should go, and even when they are old they will not turn from it." My parents were also firm believers of Proverbs 23:13, which says: "Do not withhold discipline from a child; if you punish them with the rod, they will not die."

There was a clear chain of command in our house. My mother and father were in charge, and my brothers, sisters, and I were expected to follow their rules. They also expected us to attend church and Sunday school at St. James Baptist Church in the Woodlawn neighborhood of Birmingham every week. We had to obey our teachers in school and complete our daily chores without complaining. There was a rotating schedule of chores, and we each had different duties every week. If it was my turn to wash dishes for a week, I couldn't do anything else after dinner until the dishes were clean. It was the same thing with sweeping and mopping the floors, washing and hanging out the clothes, or cleaning up the yard. If I didn't attend church on Sunday morning because I was too tired or didn't feel well, I wasn't allowed to do anything else the rest of the day. I had to stay in the house and couldn't go outside.

I didn't skip church very often, because I didn't want to miss out on playing with my friends. When I was younger, we lived in Parker Heights, which was across the street from Birmingham's airport. Our neighborhood was near Daniel Payne College, which was a historically black college until it closed in 1979. Our neighbors had seven boys, and Vince and I played sports with them as much as possible. Our backyard was about fifty feet wide and their backyard was about as big. Together, we had a 100-yard-long football field. We played football so much that we killed the grass in both yards. After a while, my dad didn't even own a lawnmower. He never complained about his grass. That's the way Pops was. He cared more about us having fun than he did about the appearance of his yard, even if some of our neighbors liked to complain about it.

When I was about seven years old, I told Pops I wanted a football of my own. At the time, he didn't have the extra money to buy me one. So he did something even better—he made one for me. Pops was taking upholstery classes at the time, and he and his instructor sewed me a cloth football and stuffed it with cotton and rags. My friends and I played with that football until the next Christmas, when I found a real one under the tree. That's what I remember most about my father. Even if he didn't have the money to buy me everything I wanted, he found a way to make me happy. Because of those long days I spent working in the cotton fields, I learned to appreciate everything my parents gave me. More than anything, I appreciated the sacrifices they made to ensure that my brothers, sisters, and I had a better life when we were adults than they'd had.

My family learned to make the most of what we had. There's no doubt in my mind that the work ethic I witnessed in my mom and dad made me a success at Woodlawn High School, the University of Alabama, and the National Football League. From an early age, my parents taught me to do my job, do it well, and not make excuses. More important, my parents taught me to respect people and treat them the way I wanted to be treated. I had no idea how valuable those lessons would be once I started attending Woodlawn High School in Birmingham.

. . . .

CHAPTER TWO

VILLAGE CREEK

Village Creek is a stream that runs for forty-four miles and snakes through the heart of Birmingham, Alabama. The creek channels through tunnels beneath Birmingham-Shuttlesworth International Airport, meanders through East Thomas Yards, North Ensley, and other parts of town, then eventually ends at a fork of the Black Warrior River.

At one time, Village Creek filled reservoirs throughout Birmingham and was the primary water source for people who lived there. During the late nineteenth century, miners pulled barges down Village Creek to carry coal. The creek is only about waist-deep, but it might as well have been as deep and wide as the Amazon River because of what it represented to my friends and me when we were growing up.

When my family lived in the Parker Heights neighborhood across from the airport, my friends and I liked to go swimming in Village Creek. Summers in Alabama were usually pretty hot and humid, and we didn't have a community swimming pool. So we'd jump into Village Creek in our blue-jean shorts to cool off. But there was a problem: Village Creek separated our all-black neighborhood from an all-white community on the other side. It was a border of sorts, and kids from both neighborhoods liked to control who swam in Village Creek.

If the white cats caught us in Village Creek, they threw stones at us to run us off. If we caught the white cats in the creek, we returned the favor by throwing rocks at them. We weren't allowed on the white side of the creek, and we expected the white kids to stay off our side, too. It wasn't that we actually hated anybody. It's the way it was back then. I didn't dislike anyone because of the color of his or her skin. I wouldn't have tried to hurt anyone, but I wasn't going to let anyone hurt me. Our battles went back and forth, and I had my share of bumps and bruises.

Growing up in Alabama during the 1960s and early 1970s,

I was aware of a lot of crazy things that were happening around me. I heard the stories about church bombings, lynchings, marches, lunch counter sit-ins, and bus boycotts during the civil rights movement. My parents tried to insulate my brothers, sisters, and me from what was happening in Birmingham. Maybe the violence was one of the reasons my parents sent us to my grandfather's farm every summer. My mom and dad knew we'd have a difficult time finding trouble—or trouble finding us—if we were in the country.

Birmingham was the battleground for the civil rights struggle. It was a dark time in America's history, and there was an international spotlight on my hometown. But I was too young to understand the magnitude of what was happening around me. I didn't realize or appreciate the sacrifices others were making to ensure that people who looked like me would have better lives in the future. And I certainly didn't know that someday I'd have a small part in making things better.

....

> Birmingham was the battleground
> for the civil rights struggle.

....

I heard about tragic incidents like the 16th Street Baptist Church bombing, which killed four young African American girls as they prepared for Sunday school on September 15, 1963. Our parents rarely took us to downtown Birmingham during that time, but I knew that was where Birmingham police commissioner Bull Connor ordered his officers to turn their water hoses and dogs on student protesters during the Children's Crusade in 1963. We were only a few miles from where everything occurred, but my parents did a good job of shielding us from the violence.

My mother attended a few civil rights meetings, and she heard Dr. Martin Luther King Jr. and other African American leaders talk about nonviolent protest. Dr. King's beliefs very much aligned with what my parents tried to teach my siblings and me. We were taught to find a peaceful resolution if we were confronted with violence. From an early age, Pops told my brothers and me to walk away if someone wanted to fight. He told us, "Don't turn your back to them, but walk away. Don't start it; but if you have to finish it, you'd better finish it." My mom was big on that one. She told us we'd better never start a fight; but if we had to use our fists, we'd sure better see it through.

When I became older, I had a difficult time understanding why racism existed. Sadly, ignorance still exists today. I never understood how someone could judge another person by the color of his or her skin. Racists don't even know me, but they judge me because I look different and am darker than they are. When people go to the beach, they're trying to look more like me. You're either born that way or trying to get that way. It's crazy.

My parents taught me to treat every man the same and never to disrespect people because of what they have or don't have. We're all different. We're not clones. My parents taught me to treat others the way I wanted to be treated. It is the Golden Rule. There is only one race on earth—and that's the human race. Even though our physical characteristics might be different, each and every one of us is equally created in the image and likeness of God. In James 2:8, God tells us that we're all equal in His eyes: "If you really fulfill the royal law according to the Scripture, 'You shall love your neighbor as yourself,' you are doing well" (ESV).

My parents instructed me to turn my head away from the racism, prejudice, and bigotry that occurred during the 1960s and early 1970s. It wasn't always easy. Pops faced discrimination while he worked in a steel mill, but he never came out and told us about the prejudice he faced. Prior to the Civil Rights Act of 1964, my father and the other African Americans who worked at the steel mill were only allowed to work as laborers, cleaning the white workers' wrenches and other tools. They earned about nine dollars per hour. Once the Civil Rights Act was passed, Pops was eligible for more skilled positions, which paid him about fourteen dollars per hour.

The only time I saw Pops upset was when one of us did something wrong. My parents always seemed to be happy, even though they dealt with the same prejudice other African Americans faced in Alabama at the time. Racism and the civil rights struggle were rarely discussed in our home. Unless one of us kids saw something on TV, my parents didn't talk about it. But they couldn't shelter us from it all the time. I remember seeing the images of violence on the TV news one night, and I asked Pops, "Why is this happening?"

"If I knew why, I would fix it," he told me. "But who knows how long it would take to fix? Some people don't like people who look different. Some people just have hatred in their hearts."

....

"If I knew why, I would fix it. Some people
just have hatred in their hearts."

....

I didn't interact with many white people until I started high school. I attended kindergarten at Groveland Baptist Church and then Bryan Elementary through the eighth grade. We didn't have middle schools back then. Bryan Elementary was an all-black school that was only a couple of miles from my parents' house, and of course Groveland Baptist church was all black.

My friends and I had to walk up a big hill to get to school. Once the school day ended, we played basketball on the playground until we had to go home to do our homework.

My friends and I also liked to play marbles. I'm a humble man, but I have to say that I was a very good marbles player. It was just a matter of being able to aim the marble where it needed to go and letting it fly. We'd draw a circle in the sand, put a line down the middle, and then play for each other's marbles. I lost a few marbles, but I usually took most of the other kids'. My favorite wins were my friends' cat's-eye marbles, which were bigger and more exotic-looking. You knew that if you walked away with somebody's prized possession, you'd had a pretty good day.

When I was young, I liked hanging out with the older kids. I thought they were more interesting, and playing sports with them was more competitive. Playing with older boys helped me improve as a baseball and basketball player. When word got around the neighborhood that I was becoming a pretty good basketball player, a few of the coaches from Huffman Park, a recreation park in Birmingham, recruited me to play on one of their teams. The coaches picked me up and brought me home every day.

Pops started coming to my basketball games, and I always knew when he was watching in the stands. As soon as I'd dribble past half-court, I'd hear him shouting, "Shoot it! Shoot it!" The only person louder in the gym was my mom. Most of my team-mates preferred playing around the basket, but I liked shooting from the perimeter. It was before the three-point rule went into effect. There's no telling how many points I might have scored if the three-pointer had been around back then. One summer, my basketball team played in a national tournament in Detroit. We won the whole thing and came home with a big trophy.

A couple of years before I started high school, Birmingham's airport authority purchased my parents' home in Parker Heights so the airport could be expanded. So in 1972 we moved to Zion City, another all-black neighborhood, which wasn't too far away from our old house. This move put me in the Woodlawn High School zoning. Birmingham's city schools were legally inte-grated in 1963, but it was two more years before African Ameri-can students attended Woodlawn High. The only thing I knew about the school was that it looked like a castle and was nicer than everywhere else I'd previously attended.

I wanted to go to Hayes High School, which was an all-black school near our neighborhood, but I was forced to go to Woodlawn High. The US Supreme Court changed every-thing in 1970 with its *Swann vs. Charlotte-Mecklenburg Board of Education* ruling, which permitted the use of busing to reach racial balance in schools across the country. I wasn't actually bused to Woodlawn High—my mom drove me to school every morning—but the government ordered me to go there against my wishes.

My aunt Erma Gean started attending Woodlawn High in 1969. Her time there didn't start very well, to say the least. Gean didn't want to be at the school, and most of the white students and teachers didn't want her there, either. Gean was a lot like my mom. She was a big, husky girl and didn't take flak from anybody. The students and teachers at Woodlawn High got to know Erma Gean very quickly. She fought anybody at the drop of a hat, and she didn't hesitate to throw a left hand. She was a southpaw, which surprised a lot of people.

I had dodged Gean's left hook quite a few times while growing up. Since she lived with our family, we had a few battles over who was the king of the crib. There were a couple of times my parents left me in charge when they were gone, and Gean tried to sneak her boyfriend into the house. I had to let her know that I was the man of the house and was in charge. Things would get interesting, to say the least. We had our moments with each other, but I loved her like a sister.

What I didn't realize until later was that Gean's quick temper helped pave the way for me to have a smoother transition into Woodlawn High. When I arrived for my freshman year in 1971, Gean had already made quite an impression. People learned that they couldn't mistreat her. They respected her—even if she had to make them respect her. The other students thought she was my sister, and people who might have messed with me thought better of it. They were like, "That's Gean's brother. Don't bother him."

Fortunately, the racial tension caused by integration had died down quite a bit by the time I arrived at Woodlawn High. But it wasn't like we were part of a big, happy student body. From my first days at the school, I had the feeling that I wasn't wanted, and I knew I didn't want to be there. However, we don't get everything we want in life, and the experience of going to a previously all-white high school was eye-opening and taught me a lot. When I walked down the hallways, a few white people looked at me as if they were amazed I was actually there. They still couldn't believe a black person was attending their school.

....

In the classrooms, the whites sat on one
side and the blacks on the other. There
was a row of seats between us.

....

At the start of the school year, police officers with dogs were stationed in hallways to deter trouble. In the beginning, you didn't want to be alone in the hallways. You always wanted your boys to be with you. For a while, the teachers and administrators let the white students go to their classes before they'd let the black students enter the hallways. In the classrooms, the whites sat on one side and the blacks on the other. There was a row of empty seats between us. It was pretty surreal.

Everything was happening so fast, and I tried to sit back and see what was going on. It was what it was. Both teachers and students treated us differently. They didn't know how to deal with us because they'd never dealt with a different race of people and didn't know anything about us. I think that might be the definition of racism—being confused about people who are different from you.

I learned a lot at Woodlawn High—but I learned more about people than I did about my school subjects. I had to figure out how to deal with others, and to give people a chance and then see how they're going to treat me. It was like learning on the job. I watched how people acted, read their demeanor, and heard what they said. Eventually, I figured out how to deal with different individuals. And, of course, there were some people I just needed to avoid.

Even some of my African American friends—people I grew up with—were racist. They didn't want to be at Woodlawn High and tried to get out. They fought anybody they could and got what they wanted—they were kicked out of school and had to go somewhere else. Racism can go both ways.

My early experiences at Woodlawn were probably different

from other African American students because I was involved in sports. Once I joined the football team, my coaches made sure I stayed out of trouble. My head coach, Tandy Gerelds, was a great man and became my father away from home. If any problems came up, I was close enough to Coach Gerelds that I could talk to him about my issues. On more than a few occasions, he told me, "Hey, you don't need to be going down that path." Fortunately, I listened to Coach and followed his lead.

We also had a rule on the football team that if a fight broke out somewhere in the school, we were supposed to leave our classes and go straight to the gym. The coaches didn't want racial problems dividing our team. The assistant coaches, like Julius Clark and Jerry Stearns, also helped me stay out of trouble. I was also close to my basketball coach, Ronnie Ryan, who helped steer me in the right direction, too.

A few of the teachers at Woodlawn High let the black students know they were there to help us. Once they figured out who we really were as individual people and that we were at Woodlawn High to do well and graduate, they wanted to help us as much as they could. I became close to a couple of the English teachers during my freshman year—Annie Bass and Joanne Ivey. Mrs. Ivey encouraged me to run for student government as a freshman. Because of my popularity as an athlete, she believed I might be able to bring the black and white students closer together. But I wasn't quite ready to get involved in something like that.

To be honest, I wasn't even sure I wanted to play football at Woodlawn High School. I'd played football with my friends in the backyard, but I'd never been part of a team in an organized league. I knew I could play the sport because I was a pretty good athlete, but I'd never been exposed to hands-on coaching, and I didn't know much about the sport's fundamentals or how to properly run offenses and defenses. But I did know one thing: I didn't want to run with the ball while other people tried to tackle me.

....

I did know one thing: I didn't want to run with
the ball while other people tried to tackle me.

....

During my freshman year, a few of my close friends decided they were going to try out for football. There weren't many African American players on the team. In fact, football had been an all-white sport at Woodlawn High School until the year before I started school there. In 1970, five black players made the school's B-team football squad. During my freshman year in 1971, five African American players—Jimmy Daniels, Rod

27

Grigsby, Rickey Jones, Gary Speers, and Steven Washington—broke the color barrier and made the varsity roster.

Since my friends decided they were going to play football, I didn't want to be left home alone with nothing to do after school. Not the highest of motivations, but it got me where I needed to be until I could find my own place and really make a difference. So, in August 1971, I walked onto a football field for my first practice at Woodlawn High School. I had no idea that my life would be changed forever.

....

CHAPTER THREE

CHICKEN BIG

When I asked my mom for permission to join Woodlawn High School's football team as a freshman, she reluctantly agreed to let me play. But she had one condition: I had to stay as far away from the football as possible. Mom didn't mind me playing sports like baseball and basketball, but she really didn't want me playing football. She didn't like the violent nature of the sport and didn't want me to be tackled by other players. Like a lot of mothers, she was worried about me getting hurt.

Once I joined the Woodlawn High School team, my mom told Coach Gerelds to put me in a position where I wouldn't have to run with the ball. During the first few practices, my teammate Denny Ragland and I battled to see who would be the freshman team's quarterback. It didn't take me long to figure out that playing quarterback in a wishbone offense wasn't what I wanted to do. In that offense, the quarterback carries the ball a lot, which means he gets tackled a lot. The physical part of the position didn't interest me. I wanted to play defense.

After a couple days of practice, Coach Gerelds did as my mother had asked and put me as far away from the football as he could. I played free safety on defense and made the B-team as a freshman. Although I had limited experience in football, my athleticism and instincts—and the great coaching I received— helped me develop into a pretty good safety rather quickly. Because of my speed, I didn't have a problem keeping up with wide receivers. And if the ball was in the air, I was going to go get it. Once a quarterback released a pass, I always felt like the ball was meant for me. It was my job to try to knock it down or pick it off.

....

Once a quarterback released a pass, I always
felt like the ball was meant for me.

....

I intercepted a few passes while playing on the B-team during my first season. Of course, as I ran for the ball while it was in the air, I could hear my mom screaming, "No! No! Don't catch it, Tony! Knock it down, baby!" Just like in my basketball games, hers was the loudest voice from the stands. It was a little embarrassing, but I loved her for it. After a few games, my mom and I reached an agreement. If I intercepted a pass, I was supposed to run straight for the sideline so I wouldn't get hit. I didn't have a problem obeying her wishes. Tackling others was much better than being tackled.

When I went out for football as a sophomore the next year, I didn't see many of my friends at the first practice. Most of my African American friends from my neighborhood had either quit or were cut from the team. I knew they were back in our neighborhood playing basketball or swimming in Village Creek without me. I didn't want to be left out, so I walked off the practice field and quit the team. But when I walked into our house, my mother saw me and stopped dead in her tracks. "Why aren't you at football practice?" she asked.

"I quit the team," I told her. "I'm not going to play football anymore."

"You did what? I've never known a Nathan to quit anything, and you're not about to become the first. Go get in the car."

My mom's reaction caught me completely by surprise.

I thought she'd be happy that I wasn't going to play football anymore. But she taught me a valuable lesson that day. She told me that if I was going to start something, no matter what it was, she expected me to finish it—there were no quitters in the Nathan house. It was a lesson that stayed with me for the rest of my life.

My mother drove me back to Woodlawn High School, where we found Coach Gerelds and the other coaches in their offices. My mom made me apologize for missing practice. Then she made me ask Coach Gerelds if he'd allow me to rejoin the team. Once Coach Gerelds agreed to have me back, my mom told him, "You do what you have to do with him as far as punishment. He's yours now. But you better make sure you keep him as far away from the football as possible."

After that conversation, it wasn't too long before the Woodlawn High School coaches started calling me "Chicken Big." They knew that I didn't like running with the football. Obviously, I wasn't very fond of the nickname. There was another guy on our team whom the coaches liked to call "Chicken Little." Since I was much bigger than he was, assistant coach Jimmy Williams started calling me "Chicken Big." Unfortunately, the coaches called me that not-so-manly name during my first couple of seasons on the team. I knew they were only having fun with me, and I actually used it as motivation to become the best player I could be.

I ended up making Woodlawn High's varsity team as a

sophomore in 1972. I was the starting free safety on defense. We opened the season against Robert E. Lee High School at the Cramton Bowl in Montgomery, Alabama. I'd never played in a stadium so large or in front of so many fans. There were probably 20,000 people there to watch us play!

I would get so nervous before a game that I'd literally lose my lunch. If the coaches couldn't find me in the locker room before a game, they usually found me hunched over a toilet in the restroom. I'd throw up before warm-ups and then come back into the locker room and get rid of everything else before the game. I was good friends with several porcelain toilets. At first, the coaches thought there was something wrong with me, but I told them it was just part of my routine and helped me get rid of the jitters. But once the team took the field and started to play, the butterflies went away and I'd be fine. But I was still a nervous wreck before every kickoff.

In the late 1960s and early 1970s, Robert E. Lee High was one of the best teams in Alabama. The Generals won back-to-back Class 4A state championships in 1969 and 1970. They were thought to be a lot better than we were in 1972; but somehow, we kept the game close, and the score was tied 3–3 in the fourth quarter. With seven minutes remaining in the game, our defense forced a fumble. I saw the ball lying on the field, ran toward it, and scooped it up. I looked up and didn't see anyone in front of me. I ran 38 yards for a touchdown. My teammate Raymond

"Buzzy" Walsh kicked the extra point and we had a 10–3 lead. Our defense intercepted two passes in the final minutes and Woodlawn won the game 10–3. It was a big upset and a huge victory for us.

Whenever Pops asked one of us about the details of a game, my mom would pipe up, "You'll have to go to the games to find out."

Unfortunately, my mom and dad weren't at the game. Well, it might have actually been a good thing that my mom didn't see me running with the ball. She might have had a heart attack in the stands! There's no telling what she might have done. She hadn't come to the game because the brakes on her car weren't working properly. Pops was out of town coon hunting, which is what he did on most weekends. When my mom heard about what I'd done, she told me she'd never miss another game—and she didn't. Pops started hearing about my plays on the field from friends at work, but Mom ordered my brothers and sisters not to tell him about what happened in the game. Whenever Pops asked one of us about the details of a game, my mom would pipe up, "You'll have to go to the games to find out."

The team won its first four games in 1972 and was ranked No. 6 in the state in Class 4A. In a 20–6 win over Ramsay High School, I intercepted three passes and made a couple of big tackles. I'm not sure how I did it, but I seemed to be in the right place at the right time. Our defense was really coming together, and guys like Steven Washington, Gary Speers, Kirk Price, and Bubba Holland did a great job of pressuring opposing quarterbacks, which made my job a lot easier. After winning our first four games, we lost to Huffman High School 20–6, but then we beat West End 20–12 at Legion Field. We had a 5–1 record going into our biggest game of the season against Banks High School at Legion Field on October 20, 1972.

The Banks High game was annually the biggest game on Woodlawn High's schedule. The only way I can describe the rivalry is that it's a lot like the Iron Bowl, in which the University of Alabama plays Auburn University every year. Fans and alumni of both schools don't like the other team, and the winner of the Iron Bowl earns bragging rights in the state for the whole next year. In Birmingham, there probably wasn't a bigger high school rivalry than Banks High and Woodlawn High. Every year, thousands of fans would fill up Legion Field to watch the schools play. Since the schools were pretty close together, a lot of my teammates grew up playing sports with guys from Banks High. Even though we were archrivals, players from both schools seemed to get along well—except for one week every year.

When we played Banks High School in 1972, the Jets were undefeated and ranked No. 1 in the state in Class 4A. The Jets had a sophomore quarterback named Jeff Rutledge, who was already one of the best players in the state. Unfortunately, Banks beat us 27–6. Although our team showed a lot of promise during my sophomore season, we knew we needed much improvement if we were going to compete with Banks—which was the best team in the city, if not the entire state. That year, the Jets finished 12–0–1 and won a state title, beating Huffman High 34–8 in the Class 4A championship game.

After losing such a big game to Banks High School, we lost two of our last three games and finished the 1972 season with a 6–4 record. It certainly wasn't the season we were hoping for after getting off to such a great start. But we were a better team and had a lot of good, young players coming back for the following season. Our prospects for 1973 were promising.

A few weeks after the 1972 season ended, Coach Gerelds approached me about moving to running back. After seeing what I did with the ball when I intercepted a pass, he thought I was a naturally gifted runner and should have the ball in my hands as much as possible. But I wanted to keep playing safety.

Even though I wasn't a blazing runner, I could make about

twenty people miss their intended passes, if I had to. And even though I didn't want to move to running back, Coach thought it was what I needed to do. I trusted Coach Gerelds enough to know he had my best interests at heart. I wanted to do whatever was needed to help the team. So I told him I'd give it a shot and see how it worked out. I know now that he saw something in me that I didn't see—or perhaps didn't want to see.

Persuading *me* to move to running back was one thing. Convincing my mother to let me do it was an entirely different matter. Coach Gerelds met with my mom and told her, "You coached him last year; I'm coaching him this year." Coach promised my mom he wouldn't run me to death and told her he would always have someone blocking for me. Somehow, Coach Gerelds persuaded my mom to let me do it. She trusted Coach and took him at his word that he'd try to protect me.

I moved to running back during spring practice before my junior season in 1973. Not all my teammates were excited about the move. We already had a couple of good running backs, and some of my teammates were not ready for an African American player to become the focal point of our offense. During the first few practices, some of my teammates decided they weren't going to block for me. I'd be lying if I said their attitude toward me didn't hurt. But I remembered what my dad told me about treating everyone with respect. It was just like when I started at

Woodlawn High—I was different. They weren't accustomed to being around me.

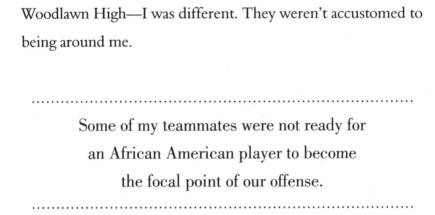

Some of my teammates were not ready for
an African American player to become
the focal point of our offense.

Moving to running back was like everything else in life—you had to earn a man's respect before he would accept you. I knew that from playing basketball. You gained respect from other players by the way you performed on the court. You didn't talk about how good you were. Instead, you played hard and to the best of your ability and let your performance do the talking. There was a lot of tension in those first few practices after I moved to tailback, but it wasn't anything I couldn't handle. I knew I was a good athlete. Once I proved I could play and showed my teammates that I was only trying to make the team better, I knew we would come together.

It also didn't hurt that one of my white teammates, Mike Allison, came to my defense during one of the first practices. I had a good relationship with Mike. He was a good person and a great football player. He was one of our starting fullbacks and a leader on defense as a linebacker. After a couple of guys failed to block for me on a running play, Mike raised his voice to get everybody's attention. Then he said that we were a team and that I was one of their teammates. He told the team that we had to come together and have better attitudes or we'd fail. After Mike's speech, guys started blocking for me on every play. I'll never forget what he did for me.

In practice, I did things I didn't know I could do. When I ran certain plays or made certain moves, I was amazed that I was doing them. Sometimes I surprised myself by the moves that came naturally to me. I found myself simply reacting to what was in front of me. In the beginning, I was worried that I might hurt the team and fumble a ball. I was happy when I wasn't the one who caused the team to lose. If I made a mistake, I'd own up to it and tell my teammates it wouldn't happen again. Then I'd work my tail off to make sure it didn't.

Coach Gerelds spent the off-season installing a revamped offense. We were moving from a wishbone offense to I-formation, which is when a fullback lines up directly in front of a tailback behind the quarterback. It's the system that college teams such as Auburn and the University of Southern California were using at the time. Auburn had a great running back named Secdrick McIntyre running the ball out of the I-formation, and guys like Joe Cribbs, James Brooks, Lionel James, and Bo Jackson came along after him. USC had unveiled the I-formation in 1963, and then Trojans tailback Mike Garrett won the Heisman Trophy as college football's best player in 1965—using the I-formation— and O. J. Simpson did the same in 1968. I was going to play the same position and run the same formation they had made famous.

My moving to tailback wasn't the only big decision my mother had to accept early in my high school career. At the beginning of my freshman year at Woodlawn, I met a girl named Johnnie Wilson. The first time I saw Johnnie, she was walking up to the second floor of the school. She was the most beautiful girl I'd ever seen. She was talking to my friend Robert Littleton. After she left, I asked Robert, "Who's that?"

I found out later that Johnnie didn't think much of me in the beginning. She described me to a mutual friend as tall, skinny, and nerdy. The first day I saw her, I was wearing a pair of plaid pants my mother had made for me, and Johnnie didn't think they were very stylish.

I also found out that Johnnie liked to hang out with a rough crowd. She was part of a group of African American students who liked to cause trouble whenever they could. They decided they were going to force white students to respect them. Johnnie lived in a neighborhood close to mine and had attended a different elementary school than I had. Her father, Harvey Wilson, was a truck driver, and her mother, Inez, was a homemaker. Johnnie had six brothers and sisters; she was the middle child.

A couple of days after seeing Johnnie for the first time, I saw her again on the second floor of the school. She captivated me. She really did. She wasn't outspoken, but she was confident. I could see it in the way she carried herself. Remember what I said about how opposites attract? I think that might be why I was so attracted to Johnnie. She is a lot like my mom and loves to talk. When Mom gets to talking, Pops sits back and listens. I'm a good listener, too—like Pops.

Johnnie did a great job of bringing me out of my shell and getting me to talk to other people. I was kind of a shy kid before I met her. She taught me that you don't have to be overbearing in your opinion, but you can state your mind.

I introduced Johnnie to my parents after a B-team football game during my freshman year. Of course, my mother immediately started asking her a thousand questions like, "Where do you live? Who are your parents? Where do you go to church?" I'm pretty sure my mother had already heard about Johnnie's reputation and probably didn't think she was the right girl for me. Honestly, my mother didn't want me having a girlfriend— period. But she invited Johnnie to go to church with our family the next Sunday, and I was happy when she showed up. She came to lunch at our house after church, and my parents were able to get to know her better.

I believe I helped Johnnie get back on the straight and narrow. She quit hanging out with her mischievous friends and started spending a lot of time with me. I learned that our upbringings were dramatically different. Johnnie likes to joke that she grew up on the wrong side of the tracks. I found out that Johnnie was dealing with some pretty serious stuff at home. Her father was on the road a lot as a truck driver; but when he was home, it wasn't pleasant. I think one of the reasons she was attracted to me was that, in my family, she saw the family she'd always wanted.

....

I grabbed her father's arm and told him, "She might be your daughter, but she's the girl I love, and this is the last time you'll ever hit her."

....

One night, I was at Johnnie's while she was washing dishes. Her father came into the kitchen and complained about the dishes not being clean enough, and he raised his hand to strike her. Looking him in the eye, I grabbed his arm and stopped him. "She might be your daughter," I said, "but she's the girl I love, and this is the last time you'll ever hit her."

Johnnie says that was the moment she fell in love with me. She knew I was the one for her because I stood up to her father to protect her. I loved Johnnie, and I wasn't going to allow her father to hurt her anymore.

Johnnie stole my heart—she really did. I salute her for weathering the storm of her family while she was growing up and getting through it. We dated for four years in high school, and then she went to college with me at the University of Alabama. We stayed together for four years in college and were eventually married in 1979.

But even before we were married and while we were in high school, Johnnie's love anchored me and helped me face situations I'd never experienced before. With all the craziness going on around me, I was happy I wasn't riding solo. Being a young man, I knew I wouldn't be perfect and wouldn't always make the right decisions; but I also knew that Johnnie would always be there to help me navigate the chaos.

Once I moved to tailback at Woodlawn High, I realized I would need all the help I could get. My world was quickly turned upside down.

CHAPTER FOUR

AMNESIA

Have you ever forgotten the details of one of the most important events of your life? My dad likes to joke that he and Mom were married on Christmas Day so he would have an easier time remembering their anniversary. Sometimes we forget a loved one's birthday or other important days, simply because the dates slip our minds. It happens to all of us from time to time.

What if I told you I don't remember much of anything about

one of the most important days of my life? Before my junior season at Woodlawn High School in 1973, Coach Tandy Gerelds decided we would have a preseason camp at the school. The camp lasted five days. Every morning, we were required to run one mile before breakfast and then we practiced three times a day. After practice was over, we ate together in the cafeteria and slept on cots in the gymnasium. It wasn't exactly how I wanted to spend the end of my summer vacation, but I was willing to do what was needed to be part of the football team.

Coach Gerelds was trying to bring us closer together through the preseason camp. Even though many of us played together the previous two seasons, there was still some racial friction on our team. Most of the guys on our team got along pretty well, whether they were black or white, but there were a few bad apples that were disrupting our team chemistry. I think Coach Gerelds figured we'd learn to get along if we spent an entire week together without any distractions.

Now, here's where my memory gets a little fuzzy. I remember my mother dropping me off at Woodlawn High School on the first day of camp. Then I remember her picking me up on Friday afternoon. But I don't remember many of the details about what happened in between. It's almost as if I had amnesia.

Unfortunately, I *did* have some sort of amnesia. I suffered a concussion during one of my first runs on the first day of camp.

I remember my head hitting the ground when I was tackled. I remember getting up and walking back to the huddle. I remember being tackled on my second run—and the back of my head hit the ground again. When we broke the huddle for a third play, I didn't react. The coaches figured out that something was wrong. The rest of the week is pretty cloudy for me.

Although I don't remember much about it, Coach Gerelds brought in a different motivational speaker every night during camp. So after dinner, our team would gather in the gymnasium, with the hopes that we would be inspired. The first night, former Woodlawn High football player David Langner spoke to us. In the spring of 1973, Langner was probably the second most famous man in the state of Alabama. Only University of Alabama coach Paul "Bear" Bryant was more recognizable. During the 1972 Iron Bowl at Legion Field in Birmingham, Alabama, Langner returned two blocked punts for touchdowns in Auburn University's 17–16 victory over Alabama. On two plays, Langner scooped up the ball and ran into the end zone after Auburn's Bill Newton blocked Greg Gantt's punts. Langner's unlikely touchdowns helped the Tigers erase a 16–3 deficit in the final ten minutes of the game. It was one of the most improbable comebacks in college football history and is still known as "Punt, Bama, Punt." Unfortunately, because of the concussion, I don't remember much of what he said.

On the second night of preseason camp, a Baptist minister spoke to us. My teammates told me his message wasn't too exciting, so when we gathered in the cafeteria for dinner on Wednesday night, there was a collective moan when Coach Gerelds informed us that *another* preacher would be speaking to us. Listening to a preacher was the last thing we wanted to do after practicing three times in the hot sun. I was exhausted and had a pounding headache. Back then, coaches and trainers didn't know what they now know about concussions. In hindsight, the practice field was probably the last place I needed to be.

There was a collective moan when Coach Gerelds informed us that *another* preacher would be speaking to us that night.

My teammates and I soon found out that Wales Goebel, the speaker, wasn't a typical preacher. He was actually an evangelist who worked with youth in Birmingham and across the South. Goebel was the son of German immigrants and grew up in Tallapoosa, Georgia. When Goebel was a teenager, he worked as a bootlegger, selling moonshine out of a taxicab. He played basketball at West Georgia College but was kicked off the team and expelled from school because he was an alcoholic. At the lowest point of his life, Goebel was invited to church by one of his friends. He became a Christian that night, and his life changed forever. After Goebel was saved, he started sharing the message of God's grace and later founded a ministry to help troubled kids.

While Goebel was leading a Bible study with football players from the University of Alabama in the spring of 1973, one of the players told him about the problems we were having at Woodlawn High School. The player told him about the racial tension at our school and the problems within our team. Goebel believed he could help us, so he showed up at Coach Gerelds's office, unannounced, during our preseason camp. He asked Coach Gerelds if he could speak to us. Apparently, Coach wasn't too interested in letting Goebel talk to us about religion. But then Goebel asked Coach Gerelds if he was certain he would go to heaven after he died. Coach Gerelds didn't know how to answer his question. He finally agreed to let Goebel talk to us for thirty minutes after dinner.

In that sweltering gymnasium, Goebel shared his story of redemption. He told us that he'd nearly been killed in a car accident and that he'd cried out to God to save him and his two friends while they were trapped in a burning car. He told us that alcoholism had nearly killed him and that his demons almost ended his relationship with the woman who had become his wife. Goebel talked to us about things like salvation and eternity and told us our lives were empty without Jesus Christ. As Goebel shared his message, a strange silence fell on the players. The bored fidgeting stopped. None of my fellow players whispered jokes or derogatory comments about the speaker. Every eye was on Goebel, and for reasons none of us understood, every heart was engaged. I now believe it was the mysterious work of God's spirit. At the end of his speech, Goebel invited anyone who wanted to become a Christian to join him on the gym floor.

One brave player stood up and then another. Slowly, my friends and teammates started making their way down the bleachers. Soon, a sea of players had joined Goebel on the floor. I was among the young men who knelt with Goebel and accepted Jesus Christ as my Lord and Savior that night.

Now, I'd be lying if I told you I actually remember going down. Coach Gerelds told me I did, Wales Goebel told me I did, and many of my teammates remember me joining them on the gymnasium floor. I may not remember the details of that night—or the entire week for that matter—but I know my life was changed. And I know that God has been directing my life and steering the wheel ever since.

....

I may not remember the details of that night,
but I know my life was changed and that God
has been directing my life ever since.

....

After that night, I witnessed dramatic changes in my coaches and teammates. Suddenly, the whole group came together in the belief that we were part of something special. In the beginning, I had my doubts about whether the changes would stick; I'm sure many of my teammates felt the same. But after that night, the changes were undeniable. We looked at each other a little differently; our attitudes changed. My own heart changed, and I saw a softer side of my teammates. After that week, we actually cared about each other. We began trusting each other, and we started working together as a team to be the best we could be. Instead of worrying about ourselves, we cared about the team as a whole and worked collectively toward a common goal.

My teammates and coaches told me I had a great time joking with my teammates and spending time with them during preseason camp. But I knew I had lost an entire week of my life, and that was a scary thing. Even so, the work God did on me that week changed my life forever—and the lives of our whole team. Amazingly, for the Woodlawn High School football team, it wasn't about black and white anymore. It was about unity.

On the night Goebel spoke to us in the gymnasium, Coach Gerelds didn't join us on the floor. I think he told a few of my teammates that he was already a Christian and didn't need to go down. It wasn't actually the truth, though. I think as our coach and leader, he didn't want us to see that he had any weaknesses. Coach Gerelds believed he had to show us that he was tough and confident.

A couple of weeks before the 1973 season started, we had a Fellowship of Christian Athletes meeting at one of my teammate's houses. His home was in an all-white neighborhood. I'd never stepped foot in that section of town before. For whatever reason, I didn't feel any anxiety about going. When I knocked on the door, his parents and my white teammates made me feel comfortable about being there. It was as if the racial barriers on our team vanished the moment we heard Goebel speak. Even though some of us looked different from others, we were now brothers working toward the same goals. That night, we read from the Bible together, sang songs, and had great fellowship.

A couple of my teammates invited Coach Gerelds to come to the meeting. Coach showed up, but he later said he hadn't felt comfortable being there. He said he felt out of place and didn't feel like he was part of our group. He stayed only for a few minutes and left. While driving home, Coach Gerelds thought about what he'd witnessed at the FCA meeting. He began to realize that he was missing something—or *Someone*—in his life, too. When Coach Gerelds walked into his bedroom that night, he fell to his knees and asked Jesus Christ to come into his heart. He became a Christian.

> Coach Gerelds spent the time and made the
> effort to make sure I didn't get into trouble.

I had a great relationship with Coach Gerelds. He was my mentor away from home. He was fair and treated us fairly. If I had an issue with someone or needed to talk to him about my problems, he was always there for me. Coach Gerelds kept me out of situations that might have caused me problems. I could have gone the other way. He spent the time and made the effort to make sure I didn't get into trouble. My mom asked him to take care of me, and he did. I respected him a great deal for doing so.

After Coach Gerelds became a Christian, we saw him smile a little bit more and his language changed. He grew as a man and in his understanding of how to deal with people. He would still put us in our place when we stepped out of line, but he knew better how to deal with individuals. He understood that some of us needed to be grabbed by the throat, while others didn't. Seeing him react to each of us according to our individual needs helped me when I started my own coaching career. You want to treat everybody the same, but you can't do it. Everybody is different, and you have to learn how to reach people in different ways.

We soon learned that Wales Goebel wasn't finished with us yet. One of the men who worked with Wales Goebel Ministries became our team chaplain. That man was Hank Erwin. At the time, I didn't know much about Hank. I knew he'd played baseball at Troy State University in Troy, Alabama. Hank walked with a limp and sometimes used a cane, because he lost part of his foot in an industrial accident. And Hank was eager to share God's Word. Sometimes, he would get so excited that he'd start stuttering when he talked. He was an excitable guy and was serious about his ministry. Hank worked hard to unite our team and bring each of us closer to Christ. Sharing the message of God's grace was Hank's mission in life, and he arrived at Woodlawn High School at the right time.

Because of my concussion, I missed nearly three weeks of practice before the 1973 season. Coach Gerelds wasn't happy about it, but he knew I couldn't risk suffering another concussion, which might have ended my football career. While I was recovering, I missed valuable practice time when I needed to be transitioning from free safety to running back. I was still learning the offense, and I needed all the carries I could get to become accustomed to running with the ball.

We opened the 1973 season against Ensley High School at Legion Field on September 7. My sophomore season had ended with a 20–6 loss to the Yellow Jackets, and our team was ready for a win.

Coach Gerelds usually addressed us before games, but this time he asked Hank to talk to us after our warm-ups. I could tell Hank was nervous—he used a baseball bat to keep his balance, and he was quite excited as he talked. He told us that no one else believed we were good enough to beat Ensley High. He told us that the *Birmingham News* picked us to win only two games the entire season. But then Hank said he believed something special was going to happen for us, because God honors those who honor Him. He asked if we were willing to believe with him.

But my career as a running back didn't get off to a grand start that night. I fumbled and turned the ball over on one of our first possessions against Ensley. Fortunately, our defense held and didn't let them score. I was happy my mistakes hadn't hurt the team. Both defenses played great and neither team scored in the first half. It was a very physical game. At halftime, Hank told us that the first half was an indication of what God could do through us—as long as we believed.

In the third quarter, I had a long punt return that set up a 29-yard field goal. We had a 3–0 lead. But late in the fourth quarter, Ensley drove 75 yards for a touchdown. We couldn't do anything on offense in the last few minutes of the game and lost 7–3. It was a heartbreaking defeat. We'd played really well on defense, certainly good enough to win the game. But we didn't do enough on offense. As we loaded onto the bus to go back to Woodlawn, I could sense that my teammates were crushed. It was a disappointing way to start the season, after we had been so excited about how our team came together during preseason camp.

As we made the drive back to our school, Hank stood up in the middle of the dark bus and spoke to us. Apparently, Coach Gerelds urged him to speak because he could sense that our hearts were aching.

....

"This is a test," Hank said, "to find out whether you are trying to use Jesus as a lucky charm, or whether you'll play for the glory of God regardless of the outcome."

....

"Now, fellas," Hank said, "I want you to understand with every commitment to Christ, there is a test to find out whether you are trying to use Jesus as a rabbit's foot or a lucky charm, or whether you really mean what you say—that you'll play for the glory of God regardless of the outcome." He paused. "This is a test to see your real motive. Did you really want Christ to be glorified, whether you won or lost, or were you using Him as a rabbit's foot or lucky charm? He has to be the Lord of all Lords. Are you totally bought in?"

One of my teammates yelled, "I'm bought in." Then somebody else said it. Instantly, the mood on the bus changed. Instead of being dejected, we were excited about how well we'd played in our first game. Nobody expected us to win, but we fought until the very end. Sure, we still had a long way to go to become a really good team, but it wasn't a bad start.

The next Monday, I was sitting alone in the bleachers at our practice field. I might have had a basketball with me, and I was thinking about what I had to do to become a better running back. I'd played okay in the first game, but I was still a bit unsure about what I was doing. Running with the ball was something that was still very new to me. As I sat there alone, Hank saw me and climbed up the bleachers. He sat down next to me and started to talk.

- -

"There's something special about you, Tony.
It's something that can't be taught. . . . And
you have to decide what to do with it."

- -

"Tony, I don't talk like Wales," Hank told me. "I don't give the big speeches, but I have something I've wanted to say to you since the first time I saw you run. There's something special about you, Tony. It's something that can't be taught. It can only be given. And you have to decide what to do with it."

I was surprised to hear what Hank was saying. I wasn't sure where our conversation was going.

"Now, when you play for yourself, you can be great," Hank said. "But when you play for a purpose higher than yourself, well, that's when extraordinary things can happen. God has a plan for your life that isn't insignificant. I can't know, of course, but I believe He wants you to be a superstar."

Could I really be great? I was too young to truly understand what Hank was saying, but it was encouraging to hear someone tell me that I had the potential to be a very good player. His words gave me the confidence I needed to take the next step as a running back.

"I'm going to tell you a secret, and I guarantee you that if you do this, you'll be a superstar in two years," Hank said.

"What is it?" I asked.

. . . .

"If you do those three things,
I guarantee you'll be a superstar."

. . . .

"One, live your life totally to serve the Lord and give Him 110 percent every day," Hank said. "You walk the talk and ask

Christ to be your Savior and the Lord of your life. You walk the talk in school, at home, and in your community. Two, you give 110 percent every day on this practice field. There can't be any slacking off; and you've got to learn your position. Third, when you play, you give it everything you have and leave only sweat on the field. If you do those three things, I guarantee you'll be a superstar."

From that day forward, I turned my life over to the Lord. I was determined to give everything I had in practice to become the best player I could possibly be. Only God knew what was going to happen to me next.

. . . .

CHAPTER FIVE

BREAKOUT

After our loss to Ensley and my "come to Jesus" discussion with Hank, my whole outlook was different. It changed how I practiced, how I played the game, how I interacted with my family, and my feelings about the racial tension in my community—and on our football team. I had promised Hank that I would give the Lord 110 percent every day, and that's what I tried to do.

Even though my time at Woodlawn High was more than

four decades ago, there are some memories that are etched into my mind forever. One of those memories is from our third game of the 1973 season. After losing to Ensley 7–3 in our season opener, we rebounded the next week and defeated Hayes High 14–3 at Lawson Field in Birmingham. Hayes High School is where I would have gone if the city's public schools hadn't been integrated, so this win was especially meaningful. Several of my friends from my old neighborhood played for the Pacemaker football team at Hayes High. I scored two touchdowns to help us win, and the newspaper said I played my best game yet.

On September 21, 1973, we played Vestavia Hills High School at Lawson Field. Vestavia Hills was a relatively new school. It opened in 1970 after many white families fled Birmingham and went "over the mountain" to the suburbs, so their children wouldn't have to attend integrated schools. The game started a lot like our first two in 1973. Even though I was feeling more confident with each game, I was still getting accustomed to playing running back. At the time, I was focused on not fumbling the ball and not hurting my team. We had a 14–7 lead at halftime, but Coach Gerelds wasn't happy with the way we'd played in the first half.

But in the third quarter—within six minutes—I scored on a 90-yard kickoff return, a 19-yard run around right end, and then a 77-yard run up the middle. I even threw a 12-yard touchdown on a trick play. We now had such a big lead that I didn't play in the fourth quarter. I finished with 410 all-purpose yards—227 rushing, 113 on two kickoff returns, 12 passing, and 58 on three punt returns.

> For the first time in my football career,
> I could envision what was coming and
> figure out how to dodge my opponents.

That night, for the first time in my football career, I could see the action playing in slow motion in my mind. I could envision what linebackers and defensive backs were going to do as they ran to tackle me, and I figured out how to dodge them and make them miss. Suddenly, something clicked in my mind and the game seemed a lot easier.

As I processed what had happened, Hank Erwin's encouragement flooded my mind. In essence, he'd said: *If you allow Christ to be the Lord of your life and if you give 110 percent in all you do, you will become a superstar.* Though I hadn't set out to be a superstar and still didn't have that as a life goal, I now felt a new purpose— even a calling—in my role as running back on the Woodlawn

High football team, and as part of the healing of the racial tension in our city.

Although everyone around me seemed amazed by the performance, I knew that our success was the result of a complete team effort. Our coach had come up with a game plan, and my teammates did a great job of reacting to whatever happened on the field and executed the game plan perfectly. My fullbacks, Mike Allison, Albert Benefield, and Peyton Zarzour, did a great job blocking for me. The offensive linemen did their jobs and opened holes for me. I've been blessed to play behind several outstanding offensive lines during my career. Those guys never get enough credit as far as I'm concerned. Our quarterback, Ronald Mumm, did a terrific job of managing the offense and making sure we were in the right plays. Before the season, Ronald was untested and inexperienced, but he ended up being the perfect quarterback for our offense in 1973. He rarely made mistakes and completed passes when we needed them.

After my final run of that game, Pops came up to the fence behind our bench. I had touched the ball only twenty times in the game, but he was worried I was going to get hurt. He spoke with conviction to Coach Gerelds: "I wouldn't plow a mule that hard. I grew up in the country and we sure didn't plow a mule like that." Pops didn't speak his mind very often, but he made his point when he did. He was always looking out for me, and I loved him for it.

The next week against Erwin High School, I ran for 203 yards and scored two touchdowns in a 21–6 victory. It was another total team effort. As a team, we were accomplishing things nobody thought we would be able to do. After the night that Wales Goebel talked to us about Jesus Christ in the gym, our team underwent a transformation. We began to care more for one another and take care of each other. Instead of playing for ourselves, we played for each other and for our coaches. We were growing into a powerful, tight-knit team.

No one outside our locker room
thought we had a chance.

After winning three of our first four games, we had to face the Vikings from Huffman High School, which was the No. 1–ranked team in the state in Class 4A. We'd lost to the Vikings 20–6 the previous year and were supposed to lose to them again. Huffman High had two great running backs, Allen Crumbley and Steve Whitman, who later played at the University of Alabama. They were great players and each skilled in their own running styles. No one outside our locker room thought we had a chance. Sure, we'd done some impressive things in our first four games, but knocking off the Vikings was an entirely different challenge.

When we boarded the bus to go to Lawson Field on October 5, 1973, our team chaplain, Hank Erwin, quieted us down. Hank talked about us being heavy underdogs and said that nobody but us believed we could win the game. Then Hank pulled out his Bible and read us the story of David and Goliath:

He said to David, "Am I a dog, that you come at me with sticks?" And the Philistine cursed David by his gods. "Come here," he said, "and I'll give your flesh to the birds and the wild animals!" David said to the Philistine, "You come against me with sword and spear and javelin, but I come against you in the name of the Lord Almighty, the God of the armies of Israel, whom you have defied. This day the Lord will deliver you into my hands, and I'll strike you down and cut off your head. This very day I will give the carcasses of the Philistine army to the birds and the wild animals, and the whole world will know that there is a God in Israel. (1 Samuel 17:43–46)

Hank told us, "You're going to win this game. You're going to win this game so people will know that there is a God in Israel."

I'd read the story of David and Goliath many times in church and Sunday school, but Hank told us that *we* could be Davids and that the Lord had the power to appoint whomever He chooses as His instrument. It was up to us, he said, to answer the calling and act on the Lord's wishes. Hank assured us that God had prepared us for the challenge we were about to face and had armed us with the necessary weapons to win. We only had to believe in ourselves—and each other—to accomplish the mighty feat.

After hearing Hank's pregame speech, we were excited about playing the game. Of course, I was nervous and spent quite a few minutes throwing up in the bathroom at Lawson Field after pregame warm-ups, as usual. The Vikings were the biggest and best team we'd played. In some ways, they looked a lot like Goliath compared to us.

Huffman High took the opening kickoff and drove 60 yards for a touchdown. The Vikings missed the extra point, so we trailed 6–0 after only a couple of minutes. After we got the ball, we faced fourth-and-one at Huffman High's 31-yard line. I took a pitch from Mumm and ran to the right side. Allison made a great block on the defensive end, which allowed me to break inside. I ran for the sideline and then broke free for a 31-yard touchdown. Buzzy Walsh made the extra-point kick, giving us a 7–6 lead. On the sideline, my teammates and coaches were going crazy. The early score gave us a lot of confidence.

After that touchdown, we became convinced we could win the game. Our safety Bobby Thompson intercepted a pass on Huffman High's next possession, which helped set up my 14-yard touchdown run on another fourth-and-one play. Then

Tommy Conwell intercepted a pass and returned it 27 yards for a touchdown to make it 20–6 at halftime. In the locker room at the half, we were bouncing off the walls with excitement. I scored two more touchdowns in the second half, and we upset the Vikings with a 35–12 victory. I finished the game with 231 rushing yards and four touchdowns—none of which would have happened without great blocking from my fullbacks and offensive line.

After the game, Hank led us in a postgame prayer. He prayed: "Lord, you have shown that it's not by power or might that we win, but it's by Your power that we win against a great giant. You've proven again tonight that there is a God in Israel."

After we beat the No. 1–ranked team in the state, the excitement surrounding our team grew tremendously in our school and around town. People talked to me and wanted to shake my hand everywhere I went. It was crazy. It was like I was in a parade, which was kind of weird for a teenager. I was only playing a game and doing what I enjoyed, but people wanted to be a part of what was going on and support us in every way. It was an amazing experience.

Back then, we wore tear-away jerseys. The flimsy jerseys ripped apart when would-be tacklers tried to grab them. When I left the field after a game, crowds gathered at the fence and in front of our locker room door. People tried to get my autograph and take photographs with me. It was nearly impossible for me to get into our locker room. My coaches and trainers came up with a solution. They started throwing parts of my tear-away jerseys into the crowd, so they'd be distracted while I went through the mob. I'd never seen anything like it, and it got a bit out of hand. I couldn't believe people could get so excited about football.

I wasn't used to receiving so much attention, and to be honest I wasn't comfortable being in the spotlight. I was a reserved person, and I hadn't had experience speaking in front of crowds and talking to the media. But I also realized that both black and white people were talking to me and trying to get close to me. I wanted to demonstrate a better way, and I hoped I showed them that regardless of skin color, we could get along. We all bleed red. Even though our skin color might be different, every one of us is human.

....

> I wanted to demonstrate a better way, and
> I hoped I showed them that regardless
> of skin color, we could get along.

....

I didn't look at myself as a freedom fighter or civil rights–movement leader. I was an athlete whom God had blessed with natural abilities. I eventually became more confident as a public speaker, and I spoke to several youth groups and churches. I tried to tell kids to be themselves, live righteously, and love one another. Coach Gerelds told me on several occasions that I could make a difference by *playing* the right way on the field and *acting* the right way off the field. He warned me that there were some people who would ask me to do things that were wrong. He told me to be myself and continue to do the right things.

About midway through my junior season, I started getting a lot of mail from college recruiters. I received letters and phone calls from recruiters from Alabama, Auburn, Georgia, Notre Dame, Oklahoma, Southern California, and Texas. The crazy thing was that I still wasn't convinced I even wanted to play football in college. I preferred playing basketball—I was an all-state guard during my junior and senior seasons—and wanted to play that sport in college. I also played baseball in high school, but preferred the faster pace of basketball and football. During my senior year, I played in an all-star baseball game at Rickwood Field in Birmingham. After the opposing pitcher struck out two batters, I hit a pitch over the tall scoreboard in center field. The game's organizers told me I would have been paid five hundred dollars if the ball had hit the clock on the scoreboard—but it flew over the clock at the top! At the very least, I wanted an opportunity to play basketball and football in college, and a few of the coaches promised me they'd give me the chance.

With so much riding on the 1973 season, I wasn't that concerned about where I was going to go to college. In my mind, that decision was still a long way off. My focus was on leading Woodlawn to a state championship. After upsetting the No. 1–ranked team in the state, we had to play No. 2 West End High School the next week. With only seven days to bounce back from the Huffman High victory, it was difficult to prepare for West End. Of course, people started telling us how great we were playing and that nobody could beat us. Coach Gerelds and our assistant coaches worked hard that week to keep us focused and grounded. We had great senior leadership in 1973, and guys like Allison, Mumm, and Zarzour prevented the rest of us from getting big heads.

As expected, the West End High game was a physical contest. We took a 7–0 lead after I scored on a nine-yard run and Walsh kicked the extra point. We didn't move the ball much the rest of the first half. West End High scored on a short touchdown pass on the final play of the half. Fortunately, our linebacker Tommy Rue blocked the extra point, allowing us to keep a 7–6 lead. At the time, we didn't know how significant that play was.

Early in the third quarter, West End scored again to take a 12–7 lead. The Lions failed to score on a two-point conversion pass, which ended up being another big play in the game. Late in the fourth quarter, we took possession at our 25-yard line. Our offensive line did a great job, and we were able to drive 80 yards for the winning touchdown. I scored on a 29-yard touchdown run, which gave us a 13–12 lead. Our defense stood up in the final minutes, and we upset a highly ranked team for the second week in a row.

Even after beating two undefeated teams in consecutive games, the biggest obstacle of our season was yet to come. We had to play Banks High School at Legion Field on October 19, 1973. Because of the way high school athletics were organized in Alabama at the time, only one of us would make the state playoffs, because we were both in the same region in Class 4A. If we defeated the Jets, there was a good chance we'd win the region and go to the playoffs. If we lost to Banks, however, we'd have to stay home for the playoffs. It basically came down to a winner-take-all contest.

Banks High School was the defending Class 4A state champion, having defeated Huffman High School 34–8 in the 1972 state title game. Their quarterback, Jeff Rutledge, was one of the best in the country. He was a heck of a player and could really throw the rock. He was a pure pocket passer and put the ball where it needed to be. Jeff earned my respect for the way he performed and led his team. He stood tall in the pocket and wasn't easily rattled.

Unfortunately for us, Jeff had plenty of help around him. Banks High School had three really good defensive ends—Bob Grefseng, Freddie Knighton, and Joe Shaw—and two really fast running backs. It was going to take our best effort of the season to beat the Jets, who were undefeated.

We got off to a great start and moved down the field during the opening kickoff. I scored on a 33-yard touchdown run to give us a quick 7–0 lead. Unfortunately, it was the last time we'd find the end zone. Banks High's defense took over and made things really difficult for us. They completely shut me down in the second half, and we lost the game 17–7. Banks High got the better of us for the second season in a row. It was a bitter pill to swallow. We were now out of the playoffs.

Banks High got the better of us for the second season in a row. It was a bitter pill to swallow.

I was proud of the way my teammates bounced back from that disappointing loss. We rebounded to beat Parker High 29–6 the next week. Our safety Bobby Thompson intercepted four passes, which was a good moment for him.

But during our next game, which was against Phillips High School, I broke my foot midway through the second quarter.

A guy grabbed my foot during a tackle, and I knew I was hurt pretty bad. With Mike Allison also on crutches on the sideline, we fell behind 13–6 late in the fourth quarter. Buzzy Walsh, who was our backup quarterback, came off the bench and threw a 37-yard pass to Mike Grauel on a Hail Mary play. Bill White, one of our backup tailbacks, scored on a one-yard run to cut the deficit to 13–12. Coach Gerelds decided to go for a two-point play to win the game, and Mumm threw a pass to Howard Ross in the end zone for a 14–13 victory. I don't think I was ever more proud of my teammates for getting the job done.

As a team, we were really banged up at the end of the 1973 season. Because my foot was still in a cast, I missed the last game against Ramsay High School on November 8. Somehow, we overcame the injuries and pulled out a 14–0 victory. We finished the season with an 8–2 record. Sure, it wasn't the magical season we were hoping for. We didn't make the playoffs and didn't beat Banks High School. But we had really come together as a team— blacks and whites. That season wasn't as much about winning games and championships as it was about changing people's mind-sets about how they treated others. It was a memorable season on the field, but I think we had an even greater impact off the field. The people of Woodlawn rallied around our team and started caring for each other, whether they were black or white.

The team had a solid nucleus coming back for the 1974 season, which would be my final campaign at Woodlawn High School. To reach our ultimate goal of making the playoffs and winning a state championship, I knew we'd have to improve during the off-season. I knew Banks High School would certainly be even better in 1974.

CHAPTER SIX

RIVALRY

There have been some great individual rivalries in sports. The feuds, vendettas, and grudge matches between athletes are some of the reasons we love to watch sports. Individual rivalries generate fans' attention, boost television ratings, and provide us with plenty of drama and excitement.

During the 1970s, one of the greatest rivalries was between boxing champs Muhammad Ali and Joe Frazier. They fought

77

three times, with the first two bouts going the distance in brutal fashion. Those guys beat the stew out of each other and really didn't like each other. After they split the first two fights, the third bout, known as the "Thrilla in Manila," was stopped after Frazier's corner wouldn't let him go out for the final round.

Larry Bird and Earvin "Magic" Johnson carried on another great rivalry. They went head-to-head in the NCAA men's basketball national championship game in 1979. Johnson led Michigan State to a 75–64 victory over Indiana State, and then Magic and Bird continued their rivalry in the NBA. During the 1980s, Johnson led the Los Angeles Lakers to five NBA championships, while Bird guided the Boston Celtics to three titles. Their teams met in the NBA finals three times, with Magic's squads winning twice. Watching those guys go head-to-head made for some of the greatest NBA games I ever saw.

Great individual rivalries—like Bill Russell versus Wilt Chamberlin in the NBA, Jack Nicklaus versus Arnold Palmer in golf, and Tom Brady versus Peyton Manning in the NFL— are what makes sports so compelling. But when fans and media become so transfixed on the individuals, they sometimes forget that the athletes are actually playing *team* sports most of the time. I know that is often the case from personal experience.

Jeff Rutledge was a great player. I found out a few
years later that Jeff was an even better person.

Entering my senior season in 1974, the preseason hype surrounding high school football in Birmingham, Alabama, wasn't
so much about Woodlawn High School versus Banks High
School as it was about Tony Nathan versus Jeff Rutledge. Jeff
was Banks High's quarterback, and he led the Jets to back-
to-back Class 4A state championships in 1972 and 1973. He was
a great player. I found out a few years later that Jeff was an even
better person, but I didn't know much about him in high school
other than that he could really throw a football.

When I began my final high school season, I wanted nothing
more than to beat Banks. My team had lost to the Jets in each of
the previous two seasons, including a bitter 17–7 defeat in 1973.
When you work as hard as we worked, it stings when you come
up short, especially when it's a loss to your biggest rival. As we
faced our senior season, Banks High was the team standing in
our way. I believed we had a chance to be one of the best teams
in the state, but we couldn't qualify for the playoffs if we didn't
defeat the Jets and win our region. We had to figure out a way to
finally beat Banks High.

The Banks-Woodlawn rivalry was intense. The rivalry began long before I started attending Woodlawn. Only a few miles separated the schools: Woodlawn was on the north side of First Avenue, and Banks was on the south side. Woodlawn High was a much older school, first opening its doors in 1916. Banks High opened in 1957 and quickly became Woodlawn High's biggest rival because of its proximity.

Even to this day, I'm glad I went to Woodlawn High instead of Banks. I'm happy my family lived on the north side of First Avenue and not the south side. There was something different about being from the south side of the street. For some reason, the people who lived on the south side believed they were better than us—maybe it was because they were richer or maybe it was because they were white. The south side of the street was predominantly white; the other side was mixed after Woodlawn High was integrated. In all of the sports we played against Banks High, we felt their arrogance. I guess I liked being at Woodlawn because I was more of an underdog. It was an interesting, healthy rivalry.

Believe it or not, I nearly ended up playing at Banks. After my freshman season at Woodlawn in 1971–72, the Birmingham Board of Education redrew its school districts and placed my neighborhood in the Banks High zone. After spending a full year getting adjusted to Woodlawn High, school officials tried to make me transfer to Banks. I didn't want to leave my school. I'd made a lot of friends on the football team, and my girlfriend attended Woodlawn. Fortunately, my parents were able to get a waiver from the school board that allowed me to stay.

Who knows how my career might have turned out if I'd attended Banks High? I might have won a couple of state championships playing with Jeff, but I wouldn't have traded my four-year experience at Woodlawn High for anything.

Rutledge was a fantastic quarterback and a big reason Banks was so good. During our senior seasons, we were both named high school All-Americans by *Family Weekly* magazine. A panel of coaches from across the country selected the team, and we were among thirty players voted to the squad. It was a big honor for both of us, and I'm sure Jeff also felt that it wouldn't have happened without the contributions of his teammates and coaches. Jeff was the centerpiece of the story, and his photograph was on the cover of millions of magazines that were included in newspapers across the country. Jeff deserved all the attention he received. He was that good. His older brother Gary played quarterback at the University of Alabama from 1972–74, and a lot of people said Jeff was even better.

Jeff and I didn't show any personal animosity toward each other. I never said anything negative about him, and he never said anything bad about me. We weren't those kinds of players or people. In fact, I never said anything bad about anyone. My newfound faith in Christ helped me keep my attitude positive. I tried to go about my business and not worry about what others said about me, but the media built up our rivalry, and it got out of hand. Of course, we were both competitors and wanted badly to win. Unfortunately, one of us was able to win more often.

Every time we played baseball or basketball against Banks High School, my teams usually won. Jeff was a great athlete and also played both of those sports. I felt great satisfaction in beating Banks High School in baseball and basketball. However, Jeff got the best of me on the football field, at least during the first two games in which we played against each other. I wanted nothing more than to beat him in my final season in 1974.

After losing to Banks High the previous two seasons, my teammates and I tried to do everything we could to make sure it didn't happen again. We spent the summer working really hard. Coach Gerelds had us go through another preseason camp—which wasn't easy, but we had a good team coming back. We added Rocha McKinstry, who hadn't played football as a junior, and he became one of our best linebackers. We lost a couple of key players, including fullback Mike Allison and quarterback Ronald Mumm. Replacing them wasn't easy. Denny Ragland took over as quarterback and was a great replacement, and Dennis Rogers and Billy Johnson became my lead blockers.

We opened the 1974 season against Ensley High School at Legion Field. Our new fullbacks and our offensive line did a great job blocking, and I finished with 266 yards and five touchdowns. It was a good way to start the season. However, I sprained my ankle on my final carry. I was worried I'd be sidelined for a few weeks, but it didn't turn out to be too bad. I came back the next week and played against Hayes. Fortunately, I didn't have to do too much. I carried the ball only four times, and we won the game 33–0. It took a few weeks for my ankle to fully recover.

....

Nothing came easy for us in 1974.

....

While our team was looking forward to the game with Banks High, we focused on our current opponent each week. Nothing came easy for us in 1974. I ran for 87 yards in a 14–0 win over Phillips High, and then 148 yards in a 14–8 victory over Vestavia Hills, which was a tough game. I was also playing safety on defense, and intercepted a pass and returned it 98 yards for a touchdown to help us beat Vestavia Hills. I was happy Coach Gerelds still gave me a chance to play on defense. I'd accepted the fact that I was probably a better running back, but I still loved playing safety.

From the start of the 1974 season, defenses started to stack the line of scrimmage to make it difficult for me. Fortunately, Denny was able to take advantage by throwing the ball down the field. After we defeated Erwin High School 20–9, Denny threw two long touchdowns in a 25–7 victory over Huffman High. He was a great leader and took control of our offense.

With a 6–0 record, we were feeling pretty good about ourselves. Our offense was getting better, and our defense was playing good football. Much like during the 1973 season, I think we were a pretty tight-knit unit. Of course, we kept an eye on what Banks was doing. The Jets were also undefeated and destroying their opponents. They won their first three games against Carver High, Hayes High, and Ramsay High by a combined score of 174–0. The Jets beat Carver High 62–0 and Hayes High 71–0. I don't think Jeff even played in the second half of any of those games!

When the Jets beat Huffman High 35–0 on October 25, 1973, they tied a city record with a 33-game streak without a defeat. Banks High hadn't lost a game since falling to Woodlawn 21–18 at the end of the 1971 season. The Jets tied Berry High 14–14 at the end of the 1972 regular season, but they'd defeated everyone else after losing to us three years earlier. They had a couple of close calls during the 1973 season, including a 7–6 victory over Ensley and an 8–6 win over Butler in the state semifinals. But

Banks High beat Grissom in the 1973 state championship game and then demolished everyone in its first eight games in 1974. I have to admit, I didn't enjoy checking the scores in the *Birmingham News* on Saturday mornings and seeing Banks win all the time.

Our goal was simple: stay undefeated until the Banks High game. After starting 6–0, we beat Ramsay High School 61–12 at Lawson Field. In that game, I somehow scored 44 points, on seven touchdowns and a two-point conversion—in less than three quarters of action. Thanks to great blocking, I ran for 228 yards on thirteen carries and returned a kickoff 87 yards for a touchdown. The performance earned me a spot in *Sports Illustrated* on November 4, 1974. I was featured in the "Faces in the Crowd" section of the magazine, which was pretty cool for a teenager. University of Oklahoma running back Joe Washington was on the cover.

My performance against Ramsay High earned me a spot in *Sports Illustrated* on November 4, 1974.

The next week against Jones Valley High, we nearly got caught looking ahead to Banks High School. We fell behind the Brownies 13–7 in the third quarter, but defensive end Brad Hendrix blocked their extra-point kick. His great play proved to be the difference for us. After Brad recovered a fumble in the fourth quarter, I scored on a 15-yard run and the extra-point kick gave us a 14–13 victory. We barely squeaked by a team we were supposed to beat soundly, but we'd accomplished what we wanted. We were 8–0 heading into the Banks High game, which would decide which team would win our region and go to the state playoffs.

Fortunately, we had two weeks to prepare for the Jets, which allowed us to get in some extra work and gave us additional time to rest and get healthy. Banks High had extended its un-beaten streak to thirty-four games. They were going to bring a twenty-four-game winning streak into our game; we'd won eleven games in a row since falling to them 17–7 during the 1973 season.

Of course, the odds were stacked against us. Banks High was a senior-laden team on both sides of the ball. Along with Rut-ledge, Jets tailbacks Jerry Murphree, Milton Miles, and Joe Wahl were seniors. Banks High also had a veteran defense, which had allowed its first eight opponents to score a total of only 33 points. We knew we were going to have a difficult time moving the ball and would have to fight for every yard. It was going to be the toughest game of our careers.

After we squeaked past Jones Valley High, the next two weeks seemed to last forever. Of course, the game was about the only thing anyone at school and around my neighborhood wanted to talk about. There was a huge buildup in the media, and stories about the game appeared in the newspapers nearly every day. The game was billed as the biggest-ever high school contest in Alabama. Naturally, everyone was talking about the Nathan-Rutledge matchup. It was crazy. Jeff had his cats, and I had mine. But we weren't playing the game by ourselves. Each team was going to win or lose together—as a team.

Woodlawn had a couple of pep rallies that week, and I could sense that Coach Gerelds was worried the buildup might be getting out of hand. I had a few sleepless nights. I badly wanted to beat Banks High. I wanted my teammates to experience what it was like to make the playoffs and win a state championship, and I have to admit that I also wanted it for me.

When the Banks High game finally arrived on November 8, 1974, it took everything I had to make it through the school day (our games were played on Thursday and Friday nights). After our pregame meal, we loaded buses to make the short drive to Legion Field. I could sense that the game was going to be much different than any contest we'd ever played. A couple of hours before the game, cars were already lined up on Graymont Avenue to get into the parking lots outside the stadium, and traffic was backed up for miles. Our team eased our way to the stadium with police escorts.

Outside Legion Field, mobs of people were lined up to get inside the gates. Several college coaches were in Birmingham to watch the game. Alabama's Bear Bryant, Auburn's Ralph "Shug" Jordan, LSU's Charlie McClendon, and a few other head coaches from Southeastern Conference schools were there. Assistant coaches from other colleges across the country also watched us play. In just a few weeks, I would have to decide where I'd play college football. But at that moment, I was focused only on leading my team to victory.

When we took the field for pregame warm-ups, I couldn't believe how many people were in the stands. I'd never seen so many people at a high school game. And I'd definitely never seen so many black and white people together. Legion Field officials estimated that 42,000 watched us play that night. The attendance set a state record for a high school game, breaking the previous mark of 32,519 when Woodlawn High played Phillips High in the 1959 Crippled Children's Classic at Legion Field. The really crazy thing is that Birmingham police estimated that another 20,000 fans couldn't get into the stadium because the lines were so long. A lot of people never even got out of their cars because they realized they couldn't get into the stadium. Legion Field officials opened only two gates to let people in;

they could have opened every gate and it might not have been enough.

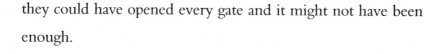

Legion Field officials estimated that 42,000 watched us play that night.

After pregame warm-ups were over, I found my favorite spot—the bathroom in our locker room. I was a nervous wreck. To make matters worse, the game was delayed twice for thirty minutes to let fans get through the gates and into their seats. I can't lie: we were nerve-racked as we waited to take the field. Usually, we sat in the locker room for twenty or thirty minutes. That night, we had to sit there for more than an hour. How hard was it to open another gate? Banks handled the delay better than we did, but that's not an excuse for the way we played.

Once the ball was finally kicked off, we got down to business. We tried to ignore the big crowd and do what we were coached to do. But I think both teams were nervous about playing in such a big game. Neither one of us moved the ball on offense in the first quarter. Our defense did a great job of putting pressure on Jeff. He hadn't played in the Jets' previous game against Jones Valley because of a badly bruised thigh. Our defensive coordinator, Jerry Stearns, decided to blitz a lot, and our defense sacked Jeff seven times. Gil Wesley, Howard Ross, and Rocha McKinstry played the games of their lives that night.

Late in the second quarter, Jeff ran an option-running play, in which the quarterback either keeps the ball or flips it to a trailing running back. He slipped a tackle and flipped the ball to Murphree, who ran for a 21-yard touchdown. The Jets missed the extra-point kick and had a 6–0 lead. We didn't do anything when we got the ball back, and then Banks needed only two plays to score again. Jeff threw a 22-yard pass to Jerry McDonald and then a 32-yard touchdown to Bob Grefseng on a busted play. It was the only touchdown catch of Grefseng's high school career. The Jets failed to convert a two-point play, so we trailed 12–0 at the half.

I have to admit that Banks High's defensive strategy that night was very good. They wanted to prevent me from getting to the sideline and did everything they could to keep me between the tackles. They did a great job of keeping the ball away from our offense. In the second half, the Jets consumed more than six minutes while driving to our 14-yard line. Somehow, our defense held them out of the end zone. But then Jeff led them on a 51-yard drive for another touchdown. Murphree scored his second touchdown on a 16-yard run, and we were behind with an 18–0 score.

We finally scored in the fourth quarter when I broke a couple of tackles and ran for a 13-yard touchdown on fourth-and-one. We kicked the point-after to make it 18–7, but it was the only time we found the end zone. Banks High won the game 18–7, beating us for the third straight season. Once again, we would have to watch the Jets make the playoffs.

....

We kicked the extra-point to make it 18–7, but it was the only time we found the end zone.

....

Our defense played well enough to win the game, but we couldn't get anything going on offense. I ended up running for 112 yards with one touchdown, but it wasn't nearly enough. We completed only one pass in the game, and Banks High's defense won the day. Making matters worse, Jeff did a fantastic job of throwing the ball, completing nine of ten passes for 185 yards with one touchdown.

In the end, both teams fell short of their goals in 1974. Banks High's 35-game winning streak ended the next week. Jeff broke his ankle in a 34–27 loss to West End High in the Jets' regular season finale, and then they fell to eventual Class 4A state champion Homewood High 12–0 in the second round of the state playoffs. That broken ankle brought a sad ending to Jeff's high school career, after he'd accomplished so much.

We rebounded to defeat Carver High School 12–0 at Lawson Field the next week. The victory gave us a 9–1 record, but we only seemed to be going through the motions after losing to Banks. It certainly wasn't the ending we were hoping for.

But that night was about more than who won the game. And it was about more than the 42,000 people who filled the stands at Legion Field and the other 20,000 who came but couldn't get in. It was about the fact that two integrated schools, each with both black and white players, battled in a stadium that was packed with black people and white people who sat with their team—not with their color. On this night, they set aside their prejudices and came together to watch a great game. Of course, the team rivalry was intense, but the rivalry was not racial. It was all about the game.

That night was a historic moment for the city of Birmingham. Birmingham had been one of the last cities to integrate its schools, and it was infamous for hate-filled violence and severe discrimination. It was in Birmingham that four young black girls were burned alive in a horrific, intentionally set church bombing. It was in Birmingham that a police commissioner turned dogs loose on children and ordered his officers to spray them with water hoses, as they peacefully demonstrated for their civil rights.

But on that night, something tangible changed in Birming-ham. That night, a divided city came together; a wounded city began to heal. After the game, white hands shook black hands and said things like, "Wow, what a game!" "Those players played their hearts out, didn't they?" "Our boys tried—they gave their best!" Black men exited the building alongside white men. Black students shared congratulations or disappointment with white students. Yes, something had definitely changed.

....

On that night, something tangible
changed in Birmingham. That night,
a wounded city began to heal.

....

Looking back on my four-year football career at Woodlawn High School, I see that time as the best four years of my life. I now believe that I was supposed to be there. I believe that being a student at Woodlawn High School and being a running back was my destiny. I believe I was there for a reason. Sure, I was able to meet new people, but more important, I accepted Jesus Christ into my life. This was when I began to play with a purpose—I was part of a team that had come together out of a commitment to Christ. I was part of a racially mixed team, and we learned to live and dream and work together.

Coach Gerelds and the other coaches nourished our love for the game and our learning to love each other. Woodlawn High School was a special place, and I was blessed to be a part of a truly special group of people and a historically significant time.

....

CHAPTER SEVEN

RECRUITING

I'll tell you one thing: after spending a few seasons working as an assistant coach and now being a college football fan, I can't figure out how high school recruits manage to survive. College recruiters, online recruiting services, and newspaper reporters from all over the country bombard them with telephone calls and e-mails. Fans on Twitter, Facebook, and other social media follow prospects' every move, from official visits to their top 10

lists of favorite schools, sometimes starting during their sophomore seasons.

When I was in high school, no one paid that much attention to college football recruiting. Sure, if you were one of the
best players, people in your hometown and maybe your home
state wanted to know where you were going to go to college.
Like they say, recruiting is the lifeblood of any college football
program, so fans are going to be interested in which players join
their favorite teams. Fortunately, the Internet wasn't around in
1974, because I'm pretty sure I wouldn't have liked having all
the attention.

About midway through my junior season at Woodlawn in
1973, cars would be lined up along our street when I came home
from football practice. College coaches were inside them, waiting for me to get home. Recruiting was a trip, man. Sometimes,
it was like we were having a house party, because there were so
many coaches there. The NCAA, which oversees college sports
and enforces its thick rulebook, didn't have as many recruiting
rules as it does now. It was like the Wild, Wild West. Coaches
didn't have a limit on how many times they could visit me.
They came as often as they wanted and stayed as long as they
liked.

Since I lived in Birmingham, the University of Alabama was
one of the first colleges that showed interest in me. My team-

mates and friends couldn't believe Crimson Tide coach Bear Bryant came to my house. They'd tell me, "Wow, Coach Bryant came to your house! He must really want you." You have to understand that Coach Bryant was a legend in the state of Alabama. After he led the Crimson Tide to three national championships during the 1960s, he may have been the most powerful man in the state. Alabama won another national title in 1973, so I was confident Coach Bryant still had what it took to win and possessed a burning desire to continue coaching. The fact that Alabama was so good also made the Crimson Tide enticing.

> Cars would be lined up along our street when
> I came home from football practice, and
> college coaches would be inside them.

Once Coach Bryant started recruiting me, he didn't pressure me to verbally commit to Alabama. In fact, he told me I could go to college wherever I wanted. But then he asked me where I wanted to live once I finished college. What Coach Bryant was telling me was that my life would be easier if I stayed home and played for the in-state school. Once I finished college, I was more likely to find a job if I played for the state school, because

Alabama alumni like to take care of their own. If I decided to attend college in California or Texas, people from Alabama may have resented me for going away to school. He also said it would be easier on my parents if I stayed close to home. If I played in Tuscaloosa, my parents wouldn't have to travel very far to watch me play.

Auburn University, the other big in-state college, also showed interest in me from the beginning. Tandy Gerelds, my coach at Woodlawn, had played baseball there and was a big Auburn football fan. I think Coach Gerelds wanted me to play for the Tigers, but he never put pressure on me. Auburn coach Shug Jordan came to my house several times and let me know he wanted me to play for him. Coach Jordan was a nice man and a good coach. He had actually coached at Auburn longer than Coach Bryant had been at Alabama. Coach Jordan was in his 23rd season at Auburn in 1973. He had guided the Tigers to a national championship in 1957, but they never seemed to win at the same level as Alabama back then. One thing working in the Tigers' favor: they also were recruiting my teammates Mike Allison and Peyton Zarzour, two of my closest friends.

There were a few other colleges I seriously considered. The University of Tennessee interested me because one of their for-mer players, Lester McClain, became like my big brother during recruiting. Lester was the first African American to play in a football game at Tennessee, breaking the color barrier during a game against the University of Georgia in 1968. Tennessee was the second school from the Southeastern Conference to integrate its football team; the University of Kentucky did it in 1967. Lester was from Nashville and was recruited by Volunteers coach Doug Dickey in 1967. The Volunteers recruited another black player that year, running back Albert Davis of Alcoa, Tennessee, but he was denied admission because of concerns about his academic records. Lester was an excellent receiver for the Volunteers, catching seventy passes for 1,003 yards with ten touchdowns from 1968 to 1970.

Lester wasn't an assistant coach at Tennessee, but he took a keen interest in my recruiting and was a big help. He was a guy I could talk with about recruiting because he'd been through the process and understood how everything worked. I also liked Tennessee because Condredge Holloway played quarterback there. Holloway became the first African American quarterback to play in the SEC, in 1972. Nicknamed the "Artful Dodger" because of his uncanny scrambling ability, Holloway could really run and throw the football. I loved watching him play. I figured if Tennessee had a black quarterback before anyone else in the South, the people there must have been somewhat forward-thinking.

During recruiting, race was an issue with a few of the schools that were talking to me. I could get a pretty good idea of how well integrated the teams were by watching how the players interacted in the locker room during my recruiting visits. At some schools, the white players sat on one side of the locker room and the blacks on the other.

Alabama was not like that. Coach Bryant came to my house and talked to me about race. He said he was running the ship and what he says goes. He promised me there would be no problems. Black players who were there at the time told me he was telling the truth. Coach Bryant didn't allow racism and prejudice to infiltrate his program. John Mitchell and Wilbur Jackson, the first two African Americans to play for the Crimson Tide, came by the house and told me everything was good. When I visited Alabama, I felt at ease. When I went down to Auburn, it was an altogether different feeling. I wasn't comfortable being there. In my first two years of high school I saw prejudice in action, and I didn't want to deal with it in college.

Tennessee was also different because of men like Lester McClain and Condredge Holloway. Bill Battle was Tennessee's coach at the time, and he wasn't afraid to play African American athletes if they deserved to play. That's the only thing I wanted—a fair opportunity to play if I was the best player at my position.

Several other colleges from around the country tried to recruit me, but I wasn't interested in going to school too far from home. I visited the University of Oklahoma, but it was too cold. The Sooners already had a great running back named Joe Washington and another one on the way: Billy Sims from Hooks, Texas, who was in the same recruiting class as me, chose to attend Oklahoma. Billy was a great running back and won the Heisman Trophy as college football's best player in 1978. It also didn't help Oklahoma's chances that Sooners coach Barry Switzer never came to Birmingham to see me. I assumed Coach Switzer really didn't want me to play there if he wouldn't take the time to meet my family.

....

Bill Battle was Tennessee's coach at the
time, and he wasn't afraid to play African
American athletes if they deserved to play.

....

When Coach Bryant came to my house, he usually wasn't alone. Most of the time, there were a few assistant coaches with him, including Jack Rutledge, Ken Donahue, and John Mitchell. Sometimes, Coach Bryant brought a couple of players with him to talk to me about what it was like at Alabama. Ozzie Newsome, who was a freshman tight end in 1974, came to my house a couple of times. Even former players like Joe Namath and Johnny Musso stopped by to see me. Coach Bryant went out of his way to make me feel like Alabama really wanted me to play there.

Of course, a few boosters also came to our house, trying to persuade me to go to their favorite schools. I didn't even know most of the cats. But they wanted to occupy my time and take care of me, whether it was by trying to take me to dinner, buying me clothes, or giving me money. I'm not going to lie: it was hard to turn down free things when people were offering them. I tried to follow recruiting rules as much as possible, but there weren't a lot of rules back then.

One thing that really upset me in high school happened when Pops bought me my first car. It was a 1964 Chevrolet Impala. Pops worked the graveyard shift at the steel mill and saved his money to buy it. However, several of my friends at Woodlawn High School teased me that a college coach gave me the car as a recruiting inducement. It really ticked me off. I can promise you one thing: if a college recruiter had bought me a car, it wouldn't have been a 1964 Impala. Don't get me wrong: I was very appreciative of Pops buying me a car. He worked hard to give it to me, and I really loved him for doing it. But if a college recruiter wanted to give me a car, it would have been a Chevrolet Chevelle SS 396. I wanted that car in burnt orange. Of course, when

I told my parents what kind of car I wanted, my momma said, "Keep on dreaming."

After being courted by college coaches for more than a year, I was ready for recruiting to end when my senior season at Woodlawn High was over. Back then, high school seniors signed with colleges shortly before Christmas Day. Now, prospects wait until the first Wednesday of February. I'm glad I didn't have to wait that long. It's a much bigger deal today than it was back then. The Birmingham newspapers and a few other media outlets around the state liked to inquire about where I was going to school, but I didn't have ESPN and other TV networks chasing me around town. The interest in high school recruiting is crazy nowadays.

When I was a senior at Woodlawn High, the signing period for Southeastern Conference schools started on December 14, 1974. I wasn't quite ready to sign a scholarship. I knew I probably wanted to attend Alabama, but I still wasn't completely sure I wanted to play football there. At the time, I thought I might play basketball for the Crimson Tide. Basketball was actually my first love and might have been my best sport. Alabama basketball coach C. M. Newton was recruiting me, but he wanted me to play both sports in college. Coach Bryant also assured me that he would give me an opportunity to play both sports if I picked the Crimson Tide.

I know my mother wanted me to choose Alabama. She loved that Coach Bryant liked to use several running backs in his offense. She didn't want me carrying the ball as much as I did in high school, especially not against the bigger, faster, and stronger defensive players I'd face in college. Tennessee's coaches promised me I would be the featured back in their offense, but I didn't think I wanted to carry the ball twenty to thirty times in a game. I wasn't sure my body could handle that kind of abuse. Sure, being the superstar would have been nice, but I may not have survived four seasons at Tennessee.

Coach Bryant also won over my dad. During one of Coach Bryant's last visits to our house, Mom cooked him one of her favorite meals: roasted raccoon. I'm pretty sure Coach Bryant had never eaten raccoon before, and his eyes became really wide when Pops informed him what we were eating for dinner that night!

....

During one of Coach Bryant's last visits
to our house, Mom cooked him one of
her favorite meals: roasted raccoon.

....

We ate raccoon a lot when I was growing up. My mom liked to parboil the raccoon in a big pot, which softens up the meat

104

but doesn't cook it completely. Then she'd either roast the raccoon with vegetables in the oven or batter it and fry it in a cast-iron skillet. Raccoon tastes pretty good when it's cleaned and cooked properly. It tastes kind of like dark meat chicken or turkey, though it's more tender than those birds when it's cooked right. Coach Bryant seemed to enjoy eating raccoon, and he later called Pops the best coon hunter in Alabama, which made my dad really proud.

That's the kind of man Coach Bryant was. He went out of his way to make others feel good, and that's one of the reasons he won over my parents and me. One of my favorite stories about Coach Bryant was a parable entitled, "It Don't Cost Nuthin' to Be Nice." Some people don't think the story is true. However, Roy Exum, a longtime sportswriter in Chattanooga, Tennessee, who covered Alabama football for years, confirmed he heard the story during a football banquet at the end of Coach Bryant's career. It goes like this:

I had just been named the new head coach at Alabama and was off in my old car down in South Alabama, recruiting a prospect who was supposed to have been a pretty good player. I was havin' trouble finding the place. Getting hungry, I spied an old cinder-block building with a small sign out front that simply said "Restaurant."

I pull up, go in, and every head in the place turns to stare at me.

Seems I'm the only white fella in the place. But the food smelled good, so I skip a table and go up to a cement bar and sit. A big ole man in a T-shirt and cap comes over and says, "What do you need?"

I told him I needed lunch and what did they have today? He says, "You probably won't like it here. Today we're having chitlins, collard greens, and black-eyed peas with cornbread. I'll bet you don't even know what chitlins are, do you?"

I looked him square in the eye and said, "I'm from Arkansas, I've probably eaten a mile of them. Sounds like I'm in the right place." They all smiled as he left to serve me up a big plate. When he comes back he says, "You ain't from around here, then?"

I explain I'm the new football coach up in Tuscaloosa at the university and I'm here to find whatever that boy's name was and he says, "Yeah, I've heard of him, he's supposed to be pretty good." And he gives me directions to the school so I can meet him and his coach.

As I'm paying up to leave, I remember my manners and leave a tip, not too big to be flashy, but a good one, and he told me lunch was on him. But I told him for a lunch that good, I felt I should pay.

The big man asked me if I had a photograph or something he could hang up to show I'd been there. I was so new that I didn't have any yet. It really wasn't that big a thing back then to be asked for, but I took a napkin and wrote his name and address on it and told him I'd get him one.

I met the kid I was lookin' for later that afternoon and I don't re-

member his name but do remember I didn't think much of him when I met him. I had wasted a day, or so I thought.

When I got back to Tuscaloosa late that night, I took that napkin from my shirt pocket and put it under my keys so I wouldn't forget it. Back then I was excited that anybody would want a picture of me. The next day, we found a picture and I wrote on it, "Thanks for the best lunch I've ever had."

Now let's go a whole bunch of years down the road. Now we have black players at Alabama and I'm back down in that part of the country scouting an offensive lineman we sure needed. Y'all remember (and I forget the name, but it's not important to the story), well anyway, he's got two friends going to Auburn and he tells me he's got his heart set on Auburn, too, so I leave empty-handed and go on to see some others while I'm down there.

Two days later, I'm in my office in Tuscaloosa and the phone rings and it's this kid who just turned me down, and he says, "Coach, do you still want me at Alabama?" And I said, "Yes, I sure do." And he says, "Okay, I'll come." And I say, "Well, son, what changed your mind?"

He said, "When my grandpa found out that I had a chance to play for you and said no, he pitched a fit and told me I wasn't going nowhere but Alabama, and wasn't playing for nobody but you. He thinks a lot of you and has ever since y'all met."

Well, I didn't know his granddad from Adam's house cat, so I asked him who his granddaddy was and he said, "You probably don't remember him, but you ate at his restaurant your first year at Alabama and you sent him a picture that he's had hung in that place ever since. That picture's his pride and joy and he still tells everybody about the day that Bear Bryant came in and had chitlins with him.

"My grandpa said that when you left there, he never expected you to remember him or to send him that picture, but you kept your word to him and, to Grandpa, that's everything. He said you could teach me more than football and I had to play for a man like you, so I guess I'm going to."

I was floored. But I learned that the lessons my mama taught me were always right. It don't cost nuthin' to be nice. It don't cost nuthin' to do the right thing most of the time, and it costs a lot to lose your good name by breakin' your word to someone.

When I went back to sign that boy, I looked up his grandpa and he's still running that place, but it looks a lot better now; and he didn't have chitlins that day, but he had some ribs that woulda made Dreamland proud, and I made sure I posed for a lot of pictures; and don't think I didn't leave some new ones for him, too, along with a signed football.

I made it clear to all my assistants to keep this story and these lessons in mind when they're out on the road. If you don't remember anything else from me, remember this. It really doesn't cost anything to be nice, and the rewards can be unimaginable.★

★Reprinted with permission from the author, Larry Burton, a longtime reporter of Alabama and SEC Football.

Isn't that the truth?

On December 14, 1974, Alabama announced its recruiting class of high school seniors. Banks High School quarterback Jeff Rutledge, who beat me three straight times, followed his older brother Gary to Alabama. Jeff was also heavily recruited by Louisiana State University, but I knew he'd probably end up playing for the Crimson Tide. Jeff was worried he wouldn't get to throw the ball much in Alabama's offense. When he asked Coach Bryant whether he'd get to throw the ball more than Alabama's previous quarterbacks if he signed with the Crimson Tide, Coach Bryant told him, "Not if we don't have to." Jeff signed with Alabama anyway. Two of Jeff's teammates at Banks High, defensive back Jerry McDonald and tackle Freddie Knighton, also signed with Alabama.

When the signing period opened, I wasn't ready to make my decision. Coach Bryant wanted to send an assistant coach to see me on the first day I could sign. I told Coach Bryant that I wanted to be alone for a few days to make a final decision. It was also my eighteenth birthday, and I wanted to celebrate with my family and Johnnie. I thought I might even wait until after basketball season to announce my college choice. But after pondering what to do for five days, I finally decided that playing football at Alabama was the best opportunity for me.

On December 19, 1974, I signed a scholarship with the

Crimson Tide during a news conference at a restaurant near Woodlawn High School. Coach Bryant and Coach Newton both attended the event, along with my family and many of my friends and teammates from Woodlawn High. It was a memorable night, and it was the end of a memorable career at Woodlawn High and the beginning of the unknown at Alabama.

....

On December 19, 1974, I signed a scholarship with the Crimson Tide during a news conference at a restaurant near Woodlawn High School.

....

I've never regretted my decision to play for the Crimson Tide. I initially chose Alabama because it was close to home and because I trusted and believed in Coach Bryant. And it didn't hurt that the Crimson Tide were usually ranked in the top five in the country at the end of the season. After coming up short in high school, I wanted a chance to win championships in college. More important, though, Coach Bryant was a lot like my father and Coach Gerelds. He was a man my parents knew they could trust to take care of me once I left home for the first time.

When I played at Alabama, Coach Bryant had two important

rules: make sure you call your momma, and go to church. Coach grew up in Arkansas and had eleven brothers and sisters. He loved his mother, Ida, and made sure we stayed in touch with our mommas while we were at school. While Coach Bryant was recruiting us, he promised our mothers that he'd make sure we attended church while we were away from home. He took that promise to heart and was a big believer in keeping his word to our mommas. We heard those rules a lot from the man, and they were probably the two biggest rules he had. Quite a few players made sure they went to church every Sunday, and I was one of them.

Coach Bryant had a strong Christian faith and felt that believing in the Lord would make you a better person inside. If in your heart you were okay with the man upstairs, Coach Bryant believed you'd be a pretty good guy. He knew that a man who didn't believe in something would fall for anything.

I wasn't alone in my Christian walk at Alabama. My mother, father, and grandparents were with me in spirit the entire time. I didn't stray far from the path because of my upbringing. It always seemed that anytime I was tempted to do something wrong, somebody or something pulled me back the other way. I realize now that I wasn't alone when I'd make a decision to stop and think twice about doing something foolish. I know now that the Lord was looking out for me. When I battled outside influences or temptations, there always seemed to be a voice telling me to stop at the moment of truth.

That voice has been with me for most of my life. When I was coaching in college and the NFL, I used to tell my players, "Think twice before making a decision. If you have a second thought about doing something, don't do it. If the Lord puts that doubt in your mind—that second thought—be cautious about what you are thinking about doing. Back away. Run away. Go the other way. Ask God to guide you, and you'll avoid a mountain of problems and consequences. Then thank Him for His help."

I learned that principle while I was in high school. When I would see questionable behavior, I'd think, "Whoa, I can't do that." I carried those strong values with me to college, and I did what Coach Bryant wanted: I went to church and I called my momma whenever I could.

Fortunately, I wasn't alone at Alabama. My girlfriend, Johnnie, joined me in Tuscaloosa, and I was so thankful to have her there with me. She was enrolled in classes and lived in a women's dormitory. I lived in a dorm with the other football players during my first couple of years.

I was thankful that I had been brought up to lean on the Lord, especially back then when I was away from home for the first time. I was taught that we all need God as our "riding partner." We have to learn to believe in Him and trust Him. As Psalm 27:1 teaches us, "The Lord is my light and my salvation—whom shall I fear? The Lord is the stronghold of my life—of whom shall I be afraid?"

As I started that new chapter in my life, God was clearly in the driver's seat.

CHAPTER EIGHT

MAGIC BANK ACCOUNT

When I started classes at the University of Alabama in August 1975, I might as well have been enrolled at the University of Southern California. Tuscaloosa was only about sixty miles from my parents' home in Birmingham, but it felt like I was as far away as the West Coast. I'd never spent much time away from my parents, brothers, and sisters, and even though Johnnie was there with me it was still somewhat unnerving to be away from my family.

I was going through the emotions every college freshman must feel. It's the first time you're away from your parents, relatives, and friends, and you're completely out of your comfort zone. But it helped that I was able to build camaraderie with my coaches and new teammates. Those relationships helped keep me from getting really homesick, but they didn't alleviate all of my anxiety.

I spent the first few weeks on the Alabama campus feeling my way around and trying to figure out where I fit in. I was able to talk to a few of my new teammates about my emotions, and they could relate. Even though Johnnie was there with me, I sometimes felt lost and would say to myself, "Good Lord, this is no-man's-land." It was all so new to me.

....

I spent the first few weeks on the Alabama
campus feeling my way around and
trying to figure out where I fit in.

....

I was blessed that I didn't have to search very far to find a church home in Tuscaloosa. My teammate Kelvin Croom's father was the pastor of College Hill Missionary Baptist Church in Tuscaloosa. Kelvin's older brother, Sylvester, was one of the first African American players to play for the Crimson Tide.

Kelvin was a running back in high school but was recruited by Alabama to play safety in the same recruiting class as me.

Sylvester and Kelvin's father, Sylvester Croom Sr., was one of the most well-respected preachers in town. He was a civil rights leader and worked with many of the students and athletes at the University of Alabama. Reverend Croom was nearly lynched when he was a boy. While he was hunting rabbits with his brothers, they got blood on their clothes. At the same time they came out of the woods, police were searching for a group of men who had raped a white girl. They assumed Reverend Croom and his brothers did it when they saw blood on their clothes. The police threw them in jail, and then an angry mob of people assembled to lynch them. Fortunately, a minister convinced the police that they had the wrong guys, and he took them to Birmingham to keep them safe. Reverend Croom and his brothers were eventually cleared as suspects.

Reverend Croom and his wife, Louise, both worked as teachers—and like my parents, they taught their sons to look beyond bigotry, ignore ignorance, and keep their anger at bay. I'm sure there were plenty of times when Kelvin and Sylvester wanted to fight back, but they always seemed to look for peaceful solutions. Reverend Croom and his wife were among the African Americans who integrated a popular restaurant in Tuscaloosa and a hotel in the state capital of Montgomery.

> There were plenty of times when Kelvin and Sylvester wanted to fight back, but they always seemed to look for peaceful solutions.

Like me, Kelvin and Sylvester had attended all-black grammar schools. The all-white Tuscaloosa Junior High School was integrated, so when they got to high school, they played football at Tuscaloosa County High School. Following a game against an all-white team, Sylvester Jr. was taunted by an angry mob. Teammates, teachers, and parents of kids from his school, both black and white, surrounded him and protected him. It helped Sylvester affirm what his parents taught him—and what my parents often told me: that there are bad people and good people, regardless of their race.

Sylvester Jr. was one of three African American players who signed to play football at the University of Alabama in 1971. Wilbur Jackson and John Mitchell became the first black players to play in a game for the Crimson Tide that same season. Sylvester Jr. played three seasons at Alabama, was named an All-American center, and voted team captain as a senior in '74. He was one of the guys I really looked up to. He later returned to Alabama and worked as an assistant for Bear Bryant. In 2003,

Sylvester Jr. was hired as Mississippi State's coach and became the first African American head coach in the seventy-one-year history of the Southeastern Conference. I couldn't have been more proud of him.

Kelvin was one of the best players in our freshman class, but he seriously injured his knee in practice in 1975. Kelvin underwent a couple of surgeries, but his knee never healed properly. He was forced to retire from football in '77. Kelvin was placed on academic scholarship, finished his undergraduate and doctorate degrees at Alabama, and became a Baptist minister. In '88, he returned to Alabama and worked as the football team's director of player development. He helped counsel student-athletes about drug and alcohol abuse and other issues. Kelvin became a school principal and eventually replaced his father as pastor of College Hill Missionary Baptist Church in Tuscaloosa. Many Alabama student-athletes still attend the church today.

Reverend Croom was an outstanding minister. He could touch your heart, and he could really bring it from the pulpit. He brought it home every Sunday. He gave me the emotional and spiritual fuel I needed to get through the next week. Reverend Croom was a big man—he was even bigger than Sylvester Jr.—and his voice boomed from the pulpit. He played football at Alabama A&M University, which is a historically black college, so I think he understood the challenges and pressures we were facing as young men and athletes. Between Reverend Croom and the choir, the services usually lasted at least two hours. I loved the music. Gospel music has a way of touching your soul.

There was an eleven o'clock service every Sunday. I usually didn't have a problem getting there, except during football season. There were times when we actually practiced on Sunday morning, especially if we didn't play well in the previous day's game. Coach Bryant wanted us to hear Reverend Croom's sermon on Sunday morning, but only after he delivered his own message to us. After beating us up for a couple of hours in practice, Coach Bryant would say, "Okay, shower up and go find a church to go to." That's the kind of man and coach he was to us.

My girlfriend, Johnnie, was also a rock about us going to church. Even if I'd returned home late from an out-of-town game on Saturday night or if I was tired and beat-up from playing, she would tell me, "Oh, no, you're getting up and going to church." No matter what time I got home on Saturday night, she'd call my phone and say, "All right, Nate, let's go."

....

No matter how tired I was, Johnnie would always say, "Oh, no, you're getting up and going to church."

....

Fellowship of Christian Athletes also had an active chapter at Alabama, and I attended several of the meetings. Several of my teammates also attended the meetings, and it was a good way for us to grow stronger in our faith together and become better teammates and friends. It was similar to the experience I had at Woodlawn High School.

I went home when I could and attended church with my family. Whenever I was feeling a little homesick, it was nice to put the Impala on the highway and head home with Johnnie. There was nothing a few nights at home and a couple of my momma's home-cooked meals couldn't cure.

Reverend Croom became more than a minister for me. He also was the football team's chaplain and was available whenever we needed him. Of course, if I really needed to talk to somebody, I called my dad. I called Pops on the phone at least once a week. Sometimes, I talked to him about the peer pressure I was facing in college. A few of the guys I hung out with liked to go to nightclubs, and a few of them liked to stir up trouble. I didn't stay in every weekend, and I wasn't perfect. I was a college kid and had my share of questionable moments. I tried to fit in, but I'd often tell my dad what was going on. His advice to me was always the same: "Be an individual, not a follower."

I did go to a few Tuscaloosa nightclubs with my buddies, but, thank God, I didn't do anything really stupid. However, we did find trouble a few times and had to pay the piper as a result. Ken Donahue, one of the assistant coaches, was in charge of handling team discipline. If we missed curfew, were caught drinking, or broke some other rule, we had to get up at six in the morning and meet him in the lower gym. He'd show up and say, "You know what you did," and then we'd take off running. We wouldn't stop until most of us were puking. He wanted the punishment to be bad enough so that we wouldn't break a rule again.

The coaches expected us to be in our rooms at ten every night. They wanted us to hang out in our rooms so we wouldn't get into trouble. In the beginning, I didn't always get in on time. But after a couple of early mornings with Coach Donahue, I learned where I needed to be and when I needed to be there. Once I found out that Billy Varner, who was Coach Bryant's bodyguard and driver, knew just about every police officer in Tuscaloosa, I decided the risk of being caught out late at night was too high. I wasn't an angel, but I never did anything too bad; I didn't want Coach Donahue knocking on my door.

One of the great things about Coach Bryant was that if you really needed something, you could go see him. He was larger than life and was the most famous man in Alabama, but he always had time for his players. He had an open-door policy and told us, "Come by when you need to. I might be busy, but I won't keep you waiting for more than ten minutes." If we told his secretary, Linda Knowles, that we needed to see Coach, she would make it happen. Like Coach Gerelds at Woodlawn, Coach Bryant was my Pops away from home. But it took me a year to muster up the courage to go see him. I was homesick and knew I could talk to him about it. We developed a great rapport.

Coach Bryant was not known as being a particularly religious person, but faith was very important to him. Not everyone knows that Coach Bryant carried a prayer in his wallet. He was known to pull it out every morning and read it when he was alone. When Coach Bryant died of a massive heart attack on January 26, 1983, a copy of the prayer was found in the back pocket of his pants.

....

What I do today is very important because
I am exchanging a day of my life for it.

....

The prayer was called "Beginning of a New Day," and he liked to read it to his players as well. The prayer goes like this:

This is the beginning of a new day. God has given me this day to use as I will. I can waste it or use it for good. What I do today is very important because I am exchanging a day of my life for it. When tomorrow comes, this day will be gone forever, leaving something in its place I have traded for it. I want it to be gain, not loss—good, not evil. Success, not failure in order that I shall not forget the price I paid for it.

When Coach Bryant died, they also found another well-worn piece of paper in his billfold. It was entitled: "The Magic Bank Account," and read:

Imagine that you had won the following prize in a contest: Each morning your bank would deposit $86,400 in your private account for your use. However, this prize has rules:

1. *Everything that you didn't spend during each day would be taken away from you.*
2. *You may not simply transfer money into some other account.*
3. *You may only spend it.*
4. *Each morning upon awakening, the bank opens your account with another $86,400 for that day.*
5. *The bank can end the game without warning: at any time it can say, "Game over!" It can also close the account and you will not receive a new one.*

What would you personally do? You would buy anything and everything you wanted, right? Not only for yourself, but for all the people you love and care for. Even for people you don't know, because you couldn't possibly spend it all on yourself, right?

You would try to spend every penny, and use it all, because you knew it would be replenished in the morning, right?

Actually, this game is real. Shocked? Yes! Each of us is already a winner of this prize. We just can't seem to see it. The prize is time.

1. *Each morning we awaken to receive 86,400 seconds as a gift of life.*
2. *And when we go to sleep at night, any remaining time is not credited to us.*
3. *What we haven't used up that day is forever lost.*
4. *Yesterday is gone forever.*
5. *Each morning the account is refilled, but the bank can dissolve your account at any time without warning.*

So, what will you do with your 86,400 seconds? Those seconds are worth so much more than the same amount in dollars. Think about it, and remember to enjoy every second of your life, because time races by much quicker than you think.

So take care of yourself, be happy, love deeply, and enjoy life!

What Coach Bryant was trying to teach us was to live every day of our lives to the fullest, because none of us are guaranteed tomorrow. We need to enjoy today, look forward to tomorrow, and forget yesterday. He wanted us to give him as much effort as we had every given day, because we can't change what we've done in the past. These were lessons I took to heart.

On the field, I had a lot to learn about football before I could earn Coach Bryant's trust in playing time. Not only did I have to learn the team's offense, but I also had to learn to block, which I'd never done much before. In high school, I was the featured running back in an I-formation. There was always a fullback in front of me, and his primary job was to block for me. My job had been to take the ball on a handoff and run. I was asked to block on a few passing plays, but quarterbacks rarely threw the ball at Woodlawn. We were a run-heavy team.

But when I arrived at Alabama in '75, the Crimson Tide had been running the wishbone offense for about four seasons. The wishbone, which puts three running backs in the backfield, debuted in college football at the University of Texas during the '68 season. Ironically, after watching Texas A&M defeat Alabama in the Cotton Bowl on New Year's Day 1968, Longhorns coach Darrell Royal instructed his offensive coordinator Emory Bellard to come up with an offense that would utilize his team's three strong running backs. Bellard came up with an altered version of the veer offense, which lined up three runners in the shape of a "Y," or a turkey wishbone. The fullback lined up right behind the quarterback, and two tailbacks split behind them. Defenses had a difficult time figuring out where the ball was going to go.

At Alabama, you had to learn how to block before the coaches gave you the privilege of running the ball. We ran the wishbone, so you had to stick your nose in the action and become a physical blocker. It was an entirely different ball game for me. I started out on the right side as a halfback during my freshman season. You had to earn the coaches' trust as a blocker before you moved to the left side.

Another big adjustment was sharing carries with so many other players. Coach Bryant liked to rotate as many as six or seven running backs in a game. It's one of the reasons my mom wanted me to play at Alabama. Coach Bryant promised her that I wouldn't be carrying the ball thirty times a game. As a freshman, I was trying to crack a very crowded backfield. Calvin Culliver was back after leading Alabama in rushing with 708 yards in 1974; fullback Johnny Davis, tailbacks Willie Shelby, Mike Stock, and others were ahead of me on the depth chart. I knew I had to work hard and become a complete running back if I was going to get on the field.

I was confident in what I could do. But there were a lot of other cats ahead of me, and they were very talented players. The coaches handed out three different colors of jerseys—red, blue, and green. Red jerseys were for the varsity players. I didn't get a red one right off the bat, but I was close. I worked with the first unit every so often during training camp in '75.

After a couple days of practice, Coach Bryant promoted Kelvin, quarterback Jeff Rutledge, and me to the varsity team. We received red jerseys and got more and more reps with the first team. I was excited to make the varsity team as a freshman, but I knew I had to keep working to stay there.

I also was excited because I was going home to play in my first college game.

CHAPTER NINE

ROLL TIDE

Once I arrived at the University of Alabama, it didn't take long for Coach Bryant to put me in my place. During a scrimmage against the second-team defense before my freshman season in 1975, I scored a touchdown on a long run. Once I reached the end zone, I started celebrating like NFL receiver Billy "White Shoes" Johnson, doing the "Funky Chicken" dance. Hey, I was excited about scoring a touchdown in college, even if it was only during an intra-squad scrimmage.

But when I reached the sideline, Coach Bryant pointed at me and said he wanted to see me.

"Son, we don't have no lightning bugs on this team," he said. "Just hand the ball to the official and act like you've been there before."

Simple enough. I left the celebrating alone after that experience. Coach Bryant told me to be humble and go to work, which is exactly what my parents taught me while I was growing up. I had a momentary lapse of judgment, and I never did it again. Coach Bryant taught me that you don't have to show your rear end to be good. He didn't want any showboats on his team, and I wasn't about to be one if he didn't want them. From that point forward, I handed the football to an official after I scored.

I was not raised to consider myself a superstar. I knew that I was only one of many players on a team, a cog in the wheel, and certainly not the key part. Some guys let the notoriety go to their heads, but Coach Bryant, my parents, and my girlfriend, Johnnie, kept me grounded. They weren't going to let me get carried away about being a running back at Alabama.

....

I knew that I was only one of many
players on a team, a cog in the wheel,
and certainly not the key part.

....

Of course, I had to wait my turn to play, which also helped keep me humble. Even though Coach Bryant liked to play a lot of running backs, there were several guys ahead of me in the pecking order. I mostly returned kickoffs during my first season, but I occasionally received some playing time at running back. Coach Bryant also let me line up at safety during a couple of preseason practices. Of course, he told me not to get comfortable on defense because I wasn't going to play on that side of the ball. It was like he was teasing me.

During my freshman season, I became good friends with Jeff Rutledge. Jeff played a lot as a freshman, and I could tell right away that he was going to be a good college quarterback. He was smart and knew how to play the game. While Jeff and I were rivals in high school, we got along great at Alabama and became good friends. Now, I didn't like talking with him about the past. The only way we talked about Banks High versus Woodlawn High was if Jeff brought it up. As the reigning football champ, he had the upper hand—no doubt about it. Although Woodlawn teams usually beat his in baseball and basketball, those victories didn't compare to his wins in football. He had bragging rights on me, for sure.

Ironically, George "Shorty" White, who coached Jeff at Banks High School, was hired by Alabama before my freshman season. As luck would have it, Coach Bryant hired him to coach the team's running backs. So the guy whose teams beat me in three straight seasons in high school was now my position coach in college. I have to be honest: I had a hard time adjusting to Coach White's coaching style. Of course, I listened to what he had to say and did what he told me to do. But at the time, I didn't give him the respect I gave Coach Bryant, Jack Rutledge, Ken Donahue, and some of the other assistants. Looking back, I realize that I hung on to what happened in high school for too long; some of the things that happened in Birmingham still bothered me. But now I understand that I should have given the man a chance.

When I arrived at Alabama, the Crimson Tide was coming off four consecutive SEC championships. Alabama went 11–1 in 1971, 10–2 in 1972, 11–1 in 1973, and 11–1 in 1974. To say Alabama fans were used to winning would have been a gross understatement. The Crimson Tide shared a national championship with Notre Dame in 1973. Back then, there were two popular polls in college football: the Associated Press top 25 and United Press International top 25. Starting in 1965, the AP waited until after postseason bowl games to vote for its national champion. The UPI did not. Alabama was ranked No. 1 in both the AP and UPI polls at the end of the 1973 season, so the UPI named the Crimson Tide its national champion. Then Notre Dame defeated Alabama 24–23 in the Sugar Bowl, so the Fighting Irish finished No. 1 in the final AP top 25. Notre

Dame also beat Alabama 13–11 in the Orange Bowl at the end of the 1974 season, costing the Crimson Tide another national title.

At the start of my freshman season, the Crimson Tide had lost only once in its last 45 regular season games. After losing to Auburn 33–28 in the Iron Bowl in 1970, Alabama's only blemish during the next four regular seasons was a 17–16 loss to Auburn in the 1972 Iron Bowl. Other than that defeat, it beat everybody else they played during the regular season for three years.

Well, Alabama's bid for a fourth perfect regular season in five years ended in my very first college game. On September 8, 1975, we opened the season against the University of Missouri at Legion Field in Birmingham. Of course, Legion Field is where I played most of my important high school games. Over the years, Alabama, Auburn, Samford University, and UAB played college football games there, along with other in-state colleges and high schools in the city. The game was played on a Monday night and televised nationally, and the Tigers absolutely manhandled us in a 20–7 loss. We fell behind quickly, so I barely even took the field in my first college game in my hometown. Missouri completely shut down our running game, holding us to 31 yards rushing, and we fell behind 20–0 at the half. Afterward, Coach Bryant said Missouri "kicked the hell out of us.

What more can I say? All in all, it was a good, old, sound country beating.

"I don't know how we'll react," Coach Bryant told reporters. "If we're the kind of people I think we are, we'll work at it and try to improve. If we don't, it will be the longest season ever around here."

We learned a valuable lesson that day—you can't take anything for granted. We were 20-point favorites over Missouri, but we simply didn't show up ready to play. Missouri ended up finishing that season with a 6–5 record. Even after all these years, I still can't believe we lost to them at home.

Fortunately, things turned around for us after that dismal beginning. After we fell from No. 2 to No. 14 in the AP poll, we blew out Clemson 56–0 at home on September 20. Jeff and I got to play together in a game for the first time, which was quite a thrill for both of us. I'm not sure what Alabama fans would have done if we'd lost a game in Tuscaloosa. It was the first game played since Alabama's stadium was renamed Bryant-Denny Stadium in honor of Coach Bryant. In his first eighteen seasons at Alabama, Coach Bryant's teams lost only once in games played at home. The Tide was 49–1 there, with the only loss coming against the University of Florida in 1963.

Our defense started playing lights-out after we lost to Missouri. Following the shutout against Clemson, we beat Vanderbilt 40–7 in Nashville, Tennessee, and then demolished Ole Miss 32–6 in Birmingham. Our defense ended up posting four shutouts during the 1975 season, and Missouri was the only team to score more than 10 points against us. With guys like Bob Baumhower, Gus White, Woodrow Lowe, and Leroy Cook causing havoc, teams had a hard time moving the ball against us.

Most of my playing time in 1975 came on special teams, whether it was returning kickoffs, covering kickoffs, or helping on punt coverage. I was happy to do whatever the team needed—I just wanted to get on the field. I did get to carry the ball sometimes. I had seven carries for 41 yards in a 52–0 rout of Washington in Tuscaloosa, which was my most extensive playing time on offense that season. It was hard to crack the running back rotation. Johnny Davis got most of the carries, and he was a big, bruising fullback. He was exactly the kind of runner you wanted in a wishbone offense. We called him "Bull" because he was so strong. Johnny had a softer side to him, though. One time, he tried to teach me how to play the piano. Apparently, my hands weren't as soft as his.

Throughout my freshman season, I tried to fit in and find my way. Even though I was on the varsity team, I didn't have much interaction with the upper classmen. But during one practice, our senior quarterback, Richard Todd, became upset about something I did. Richard had a lot of pride in his arm, so he threw the ball at me really hard. I caught it, which surprised him. "That the best you got?" I asked him. I'm pretty sure it ticked him off even more, but he left me alone after that.

....

> Richard threw the ball at me really hard.
> I caught it, which surprised him. "That
> the best you got?" I asked him.

....

After losing to Missouri, we ended up winning our next eleven games, including a 28–0 victory over Auburn in the Iron Bowl at Legion Field. It was Shug Jordan's final game as Auburn's coach. He announced his retirement before the game, and then we shut his team out in his farewell. The Auburn games were always special, particularly when we won. Coach Bryant didn't like Auburn very much, and neither did I.

When I arrived at Alabama, our poor performance in bowl games was a real source of frustration. After doing so well during the regular season, the Crimson Tide couldn't manage to win its bowl game. After Alabama defeated Nebraska 34–7 in the Sugar Bowl at the end of the 1966 season, it didn't win again in its next eight postseason appearances. Bama tied Oklahoma 24–24 in the 1970 Bluebonnet Bowl and then lost seven other times.

Once I arrived in Tuscaloosa, the bowl drought was brought to our attention, and the coaches spoke about it frequently. We were reminded of it often and didn't enjoy hearing about it. One of the goals of my recruiting class was to do something about it.

We played Penn State University in the Sugar Bowl in New Orleans on New Year's Eve 1975. There was some controversy about the matchup because Coach Bryant selected Penn State to play us, instead of a higher-ranked opponent from the Big Eight Conference or Big Ten Conference. Coach Bryant was also Alabama's athletics director at the time, so he was involved in where we played and whom we played in the postseason. Oklahoma's Barry Switzer and Nebraska's Tom Osborne gave Coach Bryant grief about his choice. I'll never forget what he said about them: "I popped off when I was young, too. To hell with them, let them go where they want to. It'll take fifteen or twenty years to get to wearing their spurs regular." Of course, Osborne and Switzer would become two of college football's most revered coaches. Back then, however, they couldn't light Coach Bryant's unfiltered Chesterfield cigarettes.

I was excited about playing in New Orleans. I'd never been there before. I hit Bourbon Street the first couple of nights, but then I shut down the fun and started concentrating on the game. I hung out on the floor of our hotel and didn't wander around town much. It was a matter of discipline. Unfortunately, several of my teammates might have had too much fun. The day before the game, Coach Bryant announced that three of our starters were going to be benched for missing our 11:00 p.m. curfew. In fact, twenty-three players missed curfew at least one night. The French Quarter was too much of a distraction for many of us.

The 1975 Sugar Bowl was the first time the game was played in the Louisiana Superdome, which opened earlier that year. I'd never played in a stadium so big. It was sort of strange looking up and seeing a roof on the stadium. When Coach Bryant led us onto the field for pregame warm-ups, he wasn't wearing his trademark houndstooth hat. He told reporters after the game that he was taught to never wear a hat indoors. He might have been trying to change our luck, too. I think Coach Bryant was willing to try anything to end our drought in bowl games. He even let his wife, Mary Harmon Bryant, ride on our team bus to the Superdome for good luck.

Before the game, Coach called us the slowest team he'd ever had at Alabama. It also didn't help that Richard Todd cut a finger on his throwing hand during Christmas break. His finger was heavily bandaged, and it was clear from the start of the game that Penn State's defense would dare him to throw. Early in the game, wide receiver Joe Dale Harris, who was thrust into the starting lineup because of the suspensions, caught a turn-in pattern and ran for a 54-yard gain. We ended up kicking a 25-yard field goal for a 3–0 lead. That was the only scoring in the first half of what was a black-and-blue, physical game.

After Penn State tied the score at 3–3 with a 42-yard field goal in the third quarter, Todd threw a long pass to tight end Ozzie Newsome. Our tailback Mike Stock scored on a 14-yard run to give us a 10–3 lead. We traded field goals with the Nittany Lions in the fourth quarter, and then our defense made a big stop at Penn State's 39-yard line with one minute, fifteen seconds to go. Finally, we had ended Coach Bryant's bowl drought with a 13–6 victory.

. . . .

Our defense made a big stop at Penn State's 39-yard line with one minute, fifteen seconds to go.

. . . .

"Lordy, it sure didn't come easy," Coach Bryant said after the game. "We beat a helluva football team tonight. Anyone who doesn't think that is an idiot."

Coach Bryant, much like my mother, was never afraid to tell you what he believed.

We finished the season with an 11–1 record and were ranked No. 3 in the final polls. It was a great way to end after the way the season started. Oklahoma won the national championship, and

Arizona State finished No. 2. Only a couple of days after football season ended, I joined Alabama's basketball team. I thought it was what I wanted to do, but I quickly realized that it would be very difficult to play both sports in college. I was tired and beat-up from football, and my teammates were all heading home until classes resumed. Plus, the guys on Alabama's basketball team were pretty good.

During the 1973–74 season, Alabama became the first team in the Southeastern Conference to start five African American players. The team was loaded with talent, including a few players I'd faced in high school. Each of the five starters from that squad ended up being drafted by NBA teams, including center Leon Douglas, who was a first-round pick of the Detroit Pistons in 1976. After watching those guys play during a couple of practices, I figured I needed to stick to football.

Not playing basketball allowed me to concentrate on preparing for my sophomore season in football. I knew I was far from a finished product. I really hit the weight room to get stronger and faster. I still had a lot to learn about playing running back in a wishbone offense. During its time, the wishbone was the offense every college team wanted to run, but it was a big adjustment for me. When I was in high school, almost everything we did in the running game occurred between the tackles. In college, it was more about getting on the edge. My running style needed to change. I was still slashing between would-be tacklers, but I had to take it wider in the wishbone.

Coach Bryant's practices were brutal, especially in the spring when we didn't have to recover quickly for games. I remember one spring practice before my sophomore season when he had the seniors out there all day long. Every day, Coach Bryant demanded that you gave him everything you had. It was a gut check for him to determine how tough we were. The games were a piece of cake compared to the practices. The practices were hard work. When we saw the defense pull out "zoot suits," which was additional padding we wore over our actual pads, we knew it was going to be a rough day.

Heading into my sophomore season in 1976, I hoped I would get to carry the ball more often on offense. We had several good running backs, including Johnny Davis, Calvin Culliver, Pete Cavan, Donald Faust, Lou Ikner, Rick Watson, and John Crow, whose father John David Crow won the Heisman Trophy at Texas A&M in 1957. John David Crow was one of Coach Bryant's assistants until he left to become the head coach at Northeast Louisiana University (now the University of Louisiana at Monroe) in 1975. With so many running backs available, I knew I was going to have to work hard to earn my opportunities.

I wish I could say that my sophomore season at Alabama started better than my freshman campaign. Unfortunately, it didn't. We opened the season against Ole Miss in Jackson, Mississippi, and fumbled the ball five times and threw three interceptions. We made too many mistakes in a 10–7 loss to the Rebels. It was the second consecutive season we'd lost our opener, and it was our first defeat in SEC play since falling to Auburn in 1972. Predictably, Coach Bryant had us practicing early on Sunday morning after that loss.

We bounced back to beat Southern Methodist University 56–3 and Vanderbilt 42–14. But then we went to Georgia, where we were embarrassed by the Bulldogs in a 21–0 loss. It was the first time one of Coach Bryant's teams was shut out since a 24–0 loss to Tennessee in 1970. Alabama went 6–5–1 that season, and after our first four games it looked like this season might be just as disappointing. After the Georgia loss, Coach Bryant took the blame for the way we played, but the defeat was on us. We didn't play well. "If the team does badly, credit me with it," Coach Bryant told reporters. "Not the players."

....

After the Georgia loss, Coach Bryant took the blame
for the way we played, but the defeat was on us.

....

We ended up losing three games during the 1976 season, and it was a nightmare. Alabama fans aren't used to losing. Notre

Dame also beat us 21–18 in South Bend, Indiana, on November 13, 1976. We had a chance to win the game, but the Fighting Irish intercepted a pass in the end zone with about four minutes to play. We had a guy open on the other side of the end zone, but Jeff didn't see him. It wasn't Jeff's fault. We made too many mistakes to win on the road. It was Alabama's third consecutive loss to Notre Dame—each of them by fewer than three points. Notre Dame seemed to have the luck of the Irish when they played us.

My offensive line played really well that day;
all I had to do was run through the holes.

It wasn't a great time for Coach Bryant. He was under a lot of pressure and scrutiny from the media and our fans. Coach Bryant was sixty-three years old and was in his 19th season coaching at Alabama. Some people started talking like he was too old and should retire. They said the same thing about him when Alabama struggled in 1969 and 1970, and the Crimson Tide won a national championship three years later. Coach Bryant had weathered the storm then, and there wasn't any doubt in my mind that he would do it again. He never showed the pressure to us. When we saw him talking on TV, we knew he wasn't happy. He didn't come out and promise that things were going to get better, but we knew they would.

Fortunately, we finished the 1976 season by winning our last two games. We beat Auburn 38–7 in the Iron Bowl at Legion Field, which quieted a lot of Coach Bryant's critics. Beating Auburn always seemed to do that. Sometimes I think that if Alabama lost eleven games in a season, its fans wouldn't care as long as Alabama defeated the Tigers. The Iron Bowl that year was my breakout game. I ran for 141 yards on twelve carries with two touchdowns. At the time, it was the fourth best rushing performance by an Alabama player against Auburn. My offensive line played really well that day; all I had to do was run through the holes. It was a lot of fun.

We ended the 1976 season by upsetting No. 5–ranked UCLA 36–6 in the Liberty Bowl in Memphis, Tennessee. UCLA had finished the regular season with a 9–1–1 record. But we were motivated to end the season on a good note and blew them out. I remember it being really, really cold in Memphis. Other than winning the game, it wasn't a great bowl experience. We were used to playing in warmer climates or inside a dome, so it was different. I managed to have a pretty good game and ran for 67 yards. Coach Bryant also let me throw a couple of passes on trick plays, including a touchdown to one of our quarterbacks, Jack O'Rear.

I'll be honest: my sophomore season wasn't much fun. It hurt. When you get a little arrogant and cocky, you don't play your best. Our fans were spoiled and so were we. But you make mistakes and try to learn from them. Obviously, we learned a lot that season. People were saying Coach Bryant's dynasty was over and that we were through. It was a matter of pride for us. We knew a three-loss season at Alabama wasn't good enough. People were looking at us differently and telling us we weren't as good as we used to be. We knew it was time to turn things around.

ABOVE: Going to midfield for the pre-game coin toss with my teammates Mike Allison (30) and Peyton Zarzour (32) before a Woodlawn High School game in 1973.

RIGHT: Taking the field with Woodlawn High School teammates Howard Ross (85), Brad Hendrix (83), and James Cottingham (61).

I'm running with the ball while wearing a tear-away jersey, which were popular in high school football during the 1970s. I went through several of them during my two seasons as a running back with the Colonels.

ABOVE: I picked up a few team awards after my junior season in 1973. My mother, Louise, tailored my pants for me.

RIGHT: While my move might have looked like the Heisman Trophy pose, I was only trying to shed a linebacker and find the end zone during a Woodlawn High School game.

Receiving an award as a defensive back at Woodlawn High School. That's defensive coordinator Jerry Stearns on my left.

Legendary Alabama coach Paul "Bear" Bryant spoke at the Woodlawn High School team banquet after my senior season in 1974.

ABOVE: Standing with Woodlawn High School coach Tandy Gerelds (far left) and several of my teammates at our team banquet in 1974.

RIGHT: My team portrait shot at Woodlawn High School during my senior season in 1974.

Coach Tandy Gerelds handing me a trophy after my senior season at Woodlawn High School in 1974.

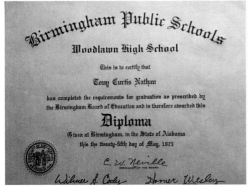

I earned my diploma from Woodlawn High School in May 1975. I earned my bachelor's degree from the University of Alabama in May 2015.

My parents—Mom (left), Coach Gerelds (middle), and my father, Pops, (right)—after I accepted a scholarship to attend the University of Alabama in December 1974.

I'm accepting a "Back of the Week" award for the Birmingham Touchdown Club. It was always an honor to be recognized in your hometown.

University of Alabama basketball coach C.M. Newton (left) and football coach Paul "Bear" Bryant (right) standing behind my parents, Pops (left) and Mom (right), after I signed with the Crimson Tide in December 1974.

Holding my younger brother Cedric at the news conference where I announced I'd play football for the Crimson Tide.

LEFT: Taking a handoff from Alabama quarterback Jeff Rutledge during a game at the University of Alabama.

RIGHT: Running the ball for Alabama against the University of Southern California in Los Angeles on October 8, 1977. It was always easier when Crimson Tide center Dwight Stephenson (57) was leading the way.

Running the ball for the Miami Dolphins in the mud against the New York Jets. Dolphins guard Jeff Toews (60) was one of the linemen who made me look good.

Johnnie and me on our wedding day at New Bethel Baptist Church in Birmingham, Alabama in 1979. We're standing with my maternal grandparents, Dorsey and Mary Williams.

One of the my best memories of coaching in the NFL was working with the NFC running backs in the 2000 Pro Bowl in Honolulu, Hawaii. Great players like Stephen Davis (48), Emmitt Smith (22), Mike Alstott (40), and Marshall Faulk (28) made my job easy.

I had the pleasure of coaching some great running backs with the Tampa Bay Buccaneers, including Jerry Ellison (37), Warrick Dunn (28), and Mike Alstott (40).

Spending time before a Tampa Bay Buccaneers game with two of the greatest influences in my life—former Buccaneers head coach Tony Dungy (middle) and former Alabama lineman Sylvester Croom (left), then an assistant with the Detroit Lions.

LEFT: I coached the Tampa Bay Buccaneers' running backs under coach Tony Dungy from 1996 to 2001.

BELOW: My daughters— Natalie, Nichole, and Nadia—with me before a Baltimore Ravens game.

Johnnie, Nichole, Natalie, and Nadia were with me when I was inducted into the Miami Dolphins' Walk of Fame in 2014.

My family had a great time visiting with ESPN broadcaster Dick Vitale and his wife, Lorraine Mc-Grath, at a fundraiser in Tampa, Florida.

Nadia, Natalie, Johnnie, and Nichole have always been my biggest fans. They attended a lot of the NFL games in which I coached.

Receiving my college diploma in May of 2015 from the University of Alabama.

....

CHAPTER TEN

REBOUND

About six months after Paul "Bear" Bryant was hired to coach football at Texas A&M University in 1954, he loaded his players on two Greyhound buses, which took them more than three hundred miles to Junction, Texas. As author Jim Dent wrote in his book *Junction Boys,* Coach Bryant took his players to "hell and back" during a weeklong training camp on the edge of Texas Hill Country. After several players quit during the camp—

which included four-hour practices three times a day with no water breaks in 110-degree heat—Bryant needed only one bus to take his team back to Texas A&M. More than twenty players quit the team, with some hitchhiking back to College Station.

After Alabama finished 9–3 during my sophomore season in 1976, we didn't receive the same harsh treatment that Texas A&M's players went through in 1954. But I have to believe what we endured might have been pretty darn close. When we started off-season conditioning drills in February 1977, the coaches turned up the heat in the lower gym. It was like a sauna. The coaches told us that if we were able to walk out of the gym, we weren't working hard enough. They wanted us crawling out. As soon as the assistant coaches walked in the door every morning, they were screaming and yelling at us. Initially, it was really difficult. But then we started helping and pushing one another. We became a much closer team as a result.

Don't get me wrong: Coach Bryant knew when to back off. Our trainer, Jim Goostree, who we called "Goose," worked for Coach Bryant for twenty-five years and was his right-hand man. Sometimes, Goose went up to Coach Bryant and said, "Coach, I think they may have had enough." On the days Coach Bryant really worked us hard in practice, Goose would tell him, "Coach, maybe take off the pads because we're out here to get in shape—not to kill each other." Most of the time, Coach Bryant listened to him. On some days, though, we almost ended up killing each other.

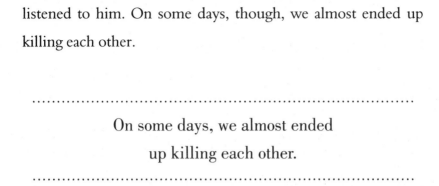

On some days, we almost ended
up killing each other.

Every now and then, Coach Bryant liked to play mind games with us. We'd think we were going to have a really hard practice, but then he'd end up sending us to the weight room and giving us the day off. Some days when we were dreading practice, he'd send us out to throw the ball around and have fun. And on a really good day, the trainers even added ice to the Gatorade. But that didn't happen often. Legend has it that a doctor once told Coach Bryant, "You don't add cold water to a hot engine. Why would you add it to a hot body?" We always had lukewarm water to drink—when we were lucky enough to get any water at all. Fortunately, Goose was always looking out for us. He'd tell Coach Bryant, "I think they need a water break." Coach Bryant would say, "Okay, if you think so."

Goose was about the same age as Coach Bryant and was a no-nonsense guy. During one practice, I was having a problem with one of my hamstrings. Goose asked me, "When does it bother you?" I told him, "Coach, I'm cool when I'm running, but when I stop it hurts." Predictably, Goose told me: "Well then, don't stop. Keep running." Goose had a deep Southern drawl and his favorite saying was: "Go put some iiiiii-ce on it."

Now, if Goose knew you were injured, you didn't practice or play in games. But if you were only hurt—and there was a big difference—there was a good chance you were going to play. You had to learn to play through bumps and bruises at Alabama. The week I had a hamstring injury, Goose came up with a crazy contraption to help me play. He taped a bicycle inner tube, of all things, to the back of my leg. Then he wrapped it around my ankle, waist, and hips. When I ran, the tube helped pull my leg up. I couldn't believe it. It worked like magic, and my hamstring didn't hurt.

One of the things that amazed me about Coach Bryant was his ability to find the right positions for players. Although I ended up staying at running back, which is where I played at Woodlawn High, he moved several of my teammates to new positions. There was no better example than Dwight Stephenson, who was a highly recruited defensive lineman from Murfreesboro, North Carolina. As soon as Dwight arrived at Alabama, Coach Bryant moved him to center. By the time Dwight was finished playing for the Crimson Tide, he was an All-American player. Coach Bryant did the same thing with Sylvester Croom, who moved to center when he was a freshman.

Dwight had a determination about him. He was a great athlete and exceptionally quick for a guy who put his hand in the dirt. Once Dwight learned the technique of playing center, he was unstoppable. After Dwight snapped the ball, he was engaged with a defensive tackle or a middle linebacker before the guy blinked. He was by far the quickest big man I've ever seen. When Dwight combined his quickness with pad level and playing with leverage, he became a very special player. Dwight also had a little finesse about him and could use a defensive guy's own movement as leverage to get the guy out of the way of the run. I'd never seen anything like it before.

··

Dwight Stephenson was by far the
quickest big man I've ever seen.

··

After we finished at Alabama, Dwight and I ended up becoming teammates again with the NFL's Miami Dolphins. He was a five-time Pro Bowler and was elected to the NFL Hall of Fame in '98. Dwight is widely regarded as the best center of his time, and he never would have played the position if Coach Bryant hadn't recognized something in him.

While Dwight was a beast on the field, he was also a very quiet guy. Alabama had quite a few players who were reserved. I think Coach Bryant wanted guys with a work ethic, who quietly went about their business. Don McNeal, one of our cornerbacks, was also like that. Dwight and Don were roommates, and they were like two peas in a pod. Don was a country bumpkin right off a farm in Atmore, Alabama. He liked to talk about his mule Kate.

Don could be put on an island to cover receivers one-on-one. He was so good in pass coverage that we could bring a safety up for run support, leaving him all alone. Don was very active out on the corner. He always seemed to cover our opponents' best receiver and usually shut him down. Don played with Dwight and me in Miami. Like me, Don played his entire NFL career with the Dolphins. He and I remain close friends. He is the pastor at New Testament Baptist Church in Coral Gables, Florida, and teaches the Sunday school class I now attend.

We had a few strange birds on our teams at Alabama. One of my roommates, Mike Coleman, was from California. He and his brother David were different cats—they were free spirits and more laid-back than the rest of us. Jim Bunch, one of our guards, always wore the same clothes: tank top, shorts, and flip-flops. He wore the same attire every day, regardless of how cold it was. The thing you have to understand is that Jim wasn't a beach bum. He was from Mechanicsville, Virginia, which isn't anywhere close to the beach. Jim was a hard-nosed football player. He liked to jump offsides, and he'd tell us he was doing it to get a defensive lineman's attention. And often, it actually worked. He'd jump offsides and whack somebody. But Coach Bryant didn't like it because his antics cost our team a five-yard penalty.

Coach Bryant always preached fundamentals. He knew that if you're a coach, you're a teacher. If you teach people the right technique, the right steps, it all comes into play. It's like putting an engine together. Coach Bryant taught work ethic and technique, and he liked to watch practice from the top of a tall tower. If we did something wrong in practice, we could hear his bullhorn hit the metal floor of the tower. It wasn't a sound you wanted to hear. The ding meant he was coming down from the tower. You'd look up and see him winding his way down the ladder. Then you'd start hoping and praying that he wasn't coming for you.

Before my junior season in '77, Johnny Davis and I were running a play in practice one day. It was an option play to the right, and I was the left halfback and Johnny didn't block his guy. The only thing we heard from the tower was: "Run it again." It happened a second time and we heard: "Run it again." Then we heard the ding. Coach Bryant came out of the tower toward us. Naturally, I moved away from Johnny a little bit. But Coach Bryant kept coming toward me, so I moved away from

Johnny again. All of a sudden, Coach Bryant grabbed Johnny by the facemask of his helmet and screamed, "You gotta block the guy! If you can't block the guy, let me know now. I'll get somebody in there who can block the guy." We ran the play again and Johnny about knocked the guy out in his block for me.

I knew one certainty while playing at Alabama: when Coach Bryant wanted to take you out, he took you out. You never knew what he was thinking. He had a plan, and it might not have been for you to stay on the field for more than two series. He was always looking ahead, trying to get people ready to play. It was never up to Shorty White, my running backs coach. Coach Bryant kept up with how many times we'd carry the ball, and then he'd tell an assistant, "Go sit him down."

In Coach Bryant's system, you had to get used to sharing the ball. In some games, you'd play the entire first quarter and then wouldn't play at all in the second. You had to get accustomed to it. I can remember running for more than 100 yards in the first half against Missouri, and then Coach Bryant told me to go sit down. I said, "Coach?" He said, "Go sit down." You had to learn the way he did things. Against Southern Methodist University during my sophomore season, we had thirteen different players run the ball. Against Vanderbilt the next week, we used eleven ball carriers. There were no superstars on Coach Bryant's teams. That was Coach Bryant's way.

One thing I eventually figured out was that when you got into a game—if you got into the game—you had to let it rip. I had a good yards-per-carry average in college because of it. I knew there was a lot of talent around me, so I had the mind-set that I had to produce every time I played. There wasn't any use in holding anything back or preserving your energy, because you weren't assured of getting back on the field. Coach Bryant always had somebody else ready to go.

....

There were no superstars on Coach Bryant's teams. That was Coach Bryant's way.

....

It's the way Coach Bryant recruited and assembled his teams. He wanted guys with a selfless attitude, who put the team ahead of themselves. The talent level around us humbled us and made us work harder. There was always competition, and the best players you faced were usually on your own team. Several of us had played against each other in high school, so we knew each other well. Coach Bryant liked to play a lot of people, and it made us a stronger team. If someone was injured, somebody else could step in and do the job. We always had legitimate depth and didn't have to use guys who hadn't been battle tested.

Heading into my junior season in 1977, I knew I'd be sharing carries with Johnny Davis, who was going to be a senior. Coach Bryant also signed a hotshot recruit named Major Ogilvie, who led Mountain Brook High School in Birmingham, Alabama, to back-to-back Class 4A state championships in 1975 and 1976. Ogilvie was big and fast, but more than anything the guy knew how to win. During preseason camp, the coaches put Major on the left side and me back on the right side. They wanted Major to learn, and he was the hot ticket. Coach had taught us to do what was best for the team, so I didn't mind seconding to Major. Major gave me some of what I gave those cats when I was a freshman.

Unlike my first two seasons at Alabama, my junior campaign got off to a fantastic start. We defeated Ole Miss 34–13 at Legion Field on September 10, 1977. It was the first time in three seasons that we won our opener. Our defense played great, shutting out the Rebels in the second half and holding them to only two first downs. Davis ran great, gaining 90 yards on eighteen carries, which helped me score two touchdowns.

Coach Bryant liked to schedule challenging nonconference games, and I'm not sure our slate could have been more difficult. We played our second game at Nebraska, which was a tough road game. It was the first time Alabama played a road contest against a Big Eight opponent. Washington State upset the Cornhuskers 19–10 in their opener, so we knew they were going to be fired up when we arrived. Plus, there was still blood boiling over what happened two years earlier, when Coach Bryant selected Penn State to play us in the Sugar Bowl, instead of Nebraska or Oklahoma. At the time, Cornhuskers coach Tom Osborne was overheard calling Coach Bryant a "son of a buck," which didn't sit well with us.

....

There was still blood boiling over what
happened two years earlier.

....

Unfortunately, Coach Osborne didn't hold anything back against us. Osborne was known as a very conservative coach, but he called three trick plays—including an I-back pass and a fake field goal—to knock us off 31–24 at Memorial Stadium. It was a big upset; we were ranked No. 4 in the country and Nebraska was unranked. Once again, our backs were against the wall early in the season. This time, though, we responded well. After losing at Nebraska, we won our next nine games to finish the regular season with a 10–1 record. We beat Vanderbilt 24–12 on the road (in gusting 30-mph winds) and then got revenge against Georgia with an 18–10 victory at Bryant-Denny Stadium in Tuscaloosa.

Because of a badly bruised thigh, I got off to a slow start that season. Fortunately, I was able to recover before we traveled to Los Angeles to play No. 1–ranked Southern California on October 8. It was my first trip to California, and it was certainly memorable. We were nine-point underdogs against the Trojans, but we played well and had a 21–6 lead midway through the fourth quarter. But then USC scored two quick touchdowns to make it 21–20 in the final minute.

With thirty-nine seconds left, Trojans coach John Robinson chose to go for a two-point conversion and a victory. Back then we didn't have overtime in college football, so the game might have ended in a tie if USC had kicked the extra point. Trojans quarterback Rob Hertel took the snap and dropped back to pass. Our defensive end Wayne Hamilton pressured him, and linebacker Barry Krauss intercepted his pass in the end zone. It wasn't the last big play Krauss would make in his Alabama career. Our 21–20 upset of the No. 1–ranked team in the country put us back in the national championship race.

After upsetting USC, we went on a roll. We beat Tennessee 24–10 at Legion Field and smoked victory cigars afterward (Goose started that tradition in the 1950s). Then we beat Louisville 55–6 in our homecoming game and trounced Mississippi State 37–7. After undefeated Michigan was upset by Minnesota, we moved to No. 2 in the Associated Press top 25 poll, behind only No. 1–ranked Texas. We remained No. 2 the next four weeks, after we defeated LSU 24–3, Miami 36–0, and Auburn 48–21 in the Iron Bowl. Our 48 points against Auburn were the most ever scored by one of Coach Bryant's teams in the Iron Bowl.

Heading into the bowl games, Texas was 11–0 and still ranked No. 1 in the AP poll. The Longhorns were going to play No. 5–ranked Notre Dame in the Cotton Bowl in Dallas. After the last weekend of the regular season, Oklahoma jumped us for No. 2 in the poll, and we dropped to No. 3 for reasons we didn't understand. Well, Texas and Oklahoma each lost badly in their bowl games. The Fighting Irish crushed the Longhorns 38–10 in the Cotton Bowl, and the Razorbacks blasted the Sooners 31–6 in the Orange Bowl. With both teams ranked ahead of us losing, you would have thought we'd finish No. 1 if we defeated Ohio State in the Sugar Bowl. While that might sound like a given to most people, that's not how college football worked back then.

We absolutely dominated Ohio State from start to finish in the Sugar Bowl on January 2, 1978. Coach Bryant decided to run right into the heart of the Buckeyes' defense, and his plan worked brilliantly as we ran for 280 yards. Ohio State's defense couldn't stop us. On our second possession, Jeff threw a 29-yard pass to Ozzie Newsome, and then I ran for a one-yard touchdown. Jeff threw a 27-yard touchdown to Bruce Bolton to give us a 13–0 lead at the half, and then he added a three-yard touchdown pass to Richard Neal and a two-point conversion to make it 21–0 in the third quarter.

The craziest thing about the Sugar Bowl is that we fumbled the ball 10 times and lost only two! I think it's safe to say the ball was bouncing our way that night. Now, we needed some luck in the polls. After the Longhorns and Sooners lost, there were five teams—Alabama, Arkansas, Notre Dame, Penn State, and Texas—that finished 11–1. The Associated Press wasn't going to release the results of its top 25 poll until the next night. I didn't see how another team would jump us after we thoroughly dominated Ohio State. Even Buckeyes coach Woody Hayes, who didn't vote in the poll (the task was left up to "unbiased" sportswriters and sportscasters), said he would have selected us as No. 1. He told reporters after the game, "I don't vote, but on the basis of what I saw tonight, Alabama would be number one. You couldn't ask a team to do more to us than they did."

Well, when the final AP top 25 poll was released on January 4, 1978, my mother heard me curse for the first time in her life. When the words rolled off my tongue, she looked at me and said, "What did you say?" We were riding in her car back to Birmingham when we heard on the radio that Notre Dame finished No. 1 in the final poll and was declared national champion. I liked to call the voters the "pipeline" because Notre

Dame always seemed to get the benefit of the doubt. Notre Dame was the only team in the country that could have jumped from No. 5 to No. 1. Everybody in America seemed to love the Fighting Irish back then. Unless you lived in Alabama, that is. In Tuscaloosa, we liked to say: "Alabama plays football, Notre Dame plays politics."

....

When the words rolled off my tongue, my mom
looked at me and said, "What did you say?"

....

There wasn't anything we could do about it. I thought we were going to win a national championship, and it broke my heart when it was taken away from us. We were ranked No. 2 in the final AP poll, only forty-eight points behind the Fighting Irish. Notre Dame received thirty-seven first-place votes, while we received nineteen.

After that Texas-size snub, I knew there was only one thing left to do: we had to win a national championship during my senior season in 1978. After getting so close in '77, we had to come back with even more hunger and motivation the next season. One thing was clear: Alabama football was back. Coach Bryant was the governor again.

. . . .

CHAPTER ELEVEN

CHAMPIONS

A dozen years before I enrolled at the University of Alabama, then Alabama governor George C. Wallace stood at the door of Foster Auditorium in a symbolic attempt to block two African American students—Vivian Malone and James Hood—from enrolling at the school. In his inauguration speech in 1963, Wallace vowed, "Segregation now, segregation tomorrow, and segregation forever." He was determined to keep students like me out of Alabama's all-white public schools and universities. It was about the same time civil rights marchers were being turned away with fire hoses and police dogs in my hometown of Birmingham. I saw some of the images on TV and never forgot them.

Before my senior season at the University of Alabama, I received the tremendous honor of being voted one of our team captains by my teammates. Quarterback Jeff Rutledge and defensive tackle Marty Lyons were also voted captains. It was kind of ironic that Jeff and I served together as captains, after we'd battled each other for three straight seasons in high school. Marty was a great defensive lineman and one of the best players on our team. He was an All American as a senior and spent eleven seasons in the NFL with the New York Jets, where he was part of the famous "New York Sack Exchange," along with Joe Klecko, Abdul Salaam, and Mark Gastineau. Being voted a captain with two guys like Jeff and Marty made the honor even more special.

A few weeks before the 1978 season started, my coaches informed me that Wallace was coming to our practice and wanted to take a photograph with the senior captains. I told my coaches that I wasn't going to take a photo with him. When I told Coach Bryant that I wasn't going to do it, he told me, "I understand." I loved him for honoring my decision and not asking me to do it. I had no respect for Wallace, who was about to end his third term as Alabama's governor. Wallace was confined to a wheelchair, after he was paralyzed from the waist down during an attempted assassination while campaigning for president in 1972.

Wallace claimed to be a born-again Christian and had previously apologized for his actions as a segregationist. He later said of his stand in the schoolhouse door, "I was wrong. Those days are over, and they ought to be over." I have to admit that I had a difficult time forgiving the man for what he'd done. At one time, Wallace believed people like me were inferior to him. He'd said people like me couldn't attend the University of Alabama, but I did anyway. As far as I was concerned, Wallace wasn't worthy of my presence for a photograph. He didn't need me, and I certainly didn't need him. I wasn't worried about hurting his feelings or doing what might have been politically correct. Jeff and Marty had their photographs taken with him, and I didn't resent them for doing it. It was their decision, and I certainly respected it. However, I didn't want to take my photo with Wallace, and I have never regretted making that decision.

Heading into my senior season, we spent quite a bit of time complaining about the poll system and how we didn't win a national championship the previous year. Much like our three-loss season in '76, we used the snub by the polls as a springboard for the next season. We wanted to get better and make sure we took the decision of who would be champion out of the hands of those who didn't vote for us. This time, we didn't want to leave any doubt. We didn't want to give voters a choice of going one way or another. The bottom line: if we took care of our business, we wouldn't have to worry about the men who voted for the national championship.

Most important, it was the last time around for the guys in my recruiting class. We wanted to go out on top of our game, so we wouldn't have regrets once we were gone. We had to make sure we were ready to play every week. Coach Bryant brought up the previous season to us quite a bit. He said, "If you leave it in somebody's hands, it's not going to turn out the way you want all the time. Go ahead and handle your business, and make up everybody's mind for them."

The 1978 season was all about everyone pulling in one direction. It was never a one-man show at Alabama. I'm not only talking about the running backs and trying to get your touches. I'm talking about the All Americans on the offensive line and on defense. There was fierce competition all over the practice field. I was one of the team leaders that year, but there were many others. I wasn't as vocal as some of them, but I did my best to lead by example. I always tried to be on time and stay out of trouble. I am not the type of person to force somebody to do something or not do something. But I tried to let the younger players know what they had to do by setting an example for them. I have never been a rah-rah guy or a vocal person. I've always let my actions speak for what I believed.

....

I wasn't as vocal as some of the team
leaders, but I tried to lead by example.

....

Our 1978 team was exceptionally close. We were a bunch of college men who were about to go our separate ways. The seniors had been together for four years. We'd gotten to know each other very well and did a lot of things together outside of football. We had cookouts and other parties at our apartments. The get-togethers weren't anything extravagant, but they brought us closer together. When it was time to play the games, we cared enough about each other to make sure we did our jobs.

I know one thing: we had to get ready in a hurry in 1978, because we weren't playing a bunch of cupcakes. Coach Bryant scheduled a brutal slate of games from the start. In the first three games we were set to play three nationally ranked opponents: Nebraska, Missouri, and Southern California. Even though we were ranked No. 1 in the polls to start the season, we knew we'd have to be ready to play. To be the best, we had to beat the best—and we were certainly going to play the best. We didn't shy away from anybody. Later, Coach Bryant admitted that he might have made a mistake scheduling so many difficult games to start the season. At the time, however, it was what it was, and we had to be ready to play.

We opened the season against No. 10–ranked Nebraska at Legion Field in Birmingham on September 2, 1978. Of course, we had revenge on our minds because the Cornhuskers were the only team to beat us the previous year. Once again, it didn't start well for us, as the Cornhuskers took an early 3–0 lead. But we responded with a 16-play, 99-yard drive in the second quarter and never looked back in a 20–3 victory.

I had a pretty good game against the Cornhuskers, running for 78 yards with one touchdown. I was also happy for Jeff. He had a rough time against Nebraska the year before, throwing five interceptions. He came back and threw for 54 yards with one touchdown and ran for 56 yards with one score. Coach Bryant didn't ask quarterbacks to do too much in our offense. If a quarterback played error-free football, he'd had a pretty good day. Jeff was nearly perfect that day.

Two weeks after beating Nebraska, we played No. 11–ranked Missouri on the road. The Tigers were sky high after upsetting Notre Dame the previous week. I'll never forget how hot it was in Columbia, Missouri. After growing up in the heat and humidity of Alabama, I thought I was ready for anything. But it was so hot—and extremely loud—at Missouri. We did a great job of quieting a record crowd of 73,655 fans by starting the game with three consecutive scores. But after we went ahead 17–0, the Tigers scored three touchdowns in less than five minutes to take a 20–17 lead at the half.

We were shell-shocked after blowing such a big lead. But Coach Bryant did a good job of getting us refocused in the locker room. After the start of the second half, one of our defensive ends, E. J. Junior, blocked a punt. Linebacker Rickey Gilliland scooped up the ball and returned it 35 yards for a touchdown, giving us a 24–20 lead. I scored on a one-yard run to make it 31–20, and then Jeff threw a 23-yard touchdown pass to Lou Ikner to give us a 38–20 victory. It was a remarkable comeback, especially on the road.

"I can remember us coming back and winning some games, but I can't remember anything that sudden happening before," Coach Bryant told reporters after the game. "It was kind of a funny atmosphere all the way around. We came out here expecting it to be cloudy and possibly rain, and it turned out sunny and as hot as a cotton patch in Arkansas."

We knew we were fortunate to win at Missouri. We were two thirds of the way through our gauntlet to start the season, but our most difficult test was yet to come. On September 23, 1978, we hosted No. 7–ranked Southern California at Legion Field. The Trojans had one of the best running backs in the country— Charles White, who would win the Heisman Trophy as college football's best player in 1979—and a very big offensive line. This time, the Trojans were looking for revenge after we knocked them off 21–20 in Los Angeles the previous season.

It ended up being a game I would like to forget. USC took an early 7–0 lead when White broke loose for a 40-yard touchdown in the first quarter. It looked like we tied the game when our freshman fullback Billy Jackson barreled into the end zone. One official ruled the play a touchdown, but another official ruled he was down at the USC one-yard line. Somehow, USC's defense stopped us four straight times, and we trailed 10–0 at the half.

In the third quarter, our halfback Major Ogilvie scored on a 31-yard touchdown to cut USC's lead to 10–7. But then the Trojans scored twice, with their second touchdown coming on a fluke play. Our cornerback Don McNeal leaped in the air to intercept a long pass, but the ball slipped through his fingers and right into the hands of Kevin Williams, who scored a 40-yard touchdown to make it 24–7. We scored quickly to cut USC's lead to 24–14, and then our defense made a big stop to get the ball back. We drove deep into USC territory, but then I fumbled after a six-yard run. We ended up losing the game 24–14.

You hate to let your teammates down, but that's what I did. I lost two fumbles in the game. Coach Bryant let me stay on the field and told me, "Don't try so hard." I was the kind of runner who liked to fight for extra yards, and that's when I fumbled. I had to learn to keep my arm where it needs to be, high and tight with the ball. You get out there and try to do some things different, and you get away from the fundamentals you've been taught. It ends up biting you. I felt awful about what happened. I felt like I'd cost my team a victory and a chance to play for a national championship. I felt like I'd cost my team a chance to win a title.

....

You hate to let your teammates
down, but that's what I did.

....

The next week, my family and friends knew I was hurting. Of course, my teammates and coaches did a great job of motivating me and keeping me focused. We had six turnovers in the game, so it wasn't entirely my fault we lost. But they had a difficult time convincing me. I was never the kind of guy who deflected blame to someone else. You have to admit your errors, realize what they were, and correct them.

If you can look in the mirror and be happy with what you see, you're good. But if you look in the mirror and justify bad things or blame other people, that's not good. The worst thing a man can do is lie to himself. Own up to your mistakes, and the Good Lord will give you the next day to get it straightened out. As a senior, I had to prove that I could bounce back. I knew Coach Bryant was going to give me a chance to come back and play. That was one of his strengths. He wouldn't push a guy to the side and forget about him because he'd made a mistake.

After losing to Southern California, we fell from No. 1 to No. 7 in the polls. We weren't entirely out of the national championship race, but we knew we couldn't afford another setback. We also knew we probably needed some help from other teams to get back to No. 1. It took us a while to get over the USC loss. I wasn't even sure I was going to play the next week against Vanderbilt because of a badly bruised shoulder. But Coach Bryant put me in the starting lineup. I think he wanted to restore my confidence. We didn't play very well against Vanderbilt and trailed 21–16 in the third quarter. But after I scored on a 63-yard touchdown run, we scored four more touchdowns to blow out the Commodores 51–28. Thanks to our great blocking up front, I finished with 163 yards on seven carries, which made me feel a lot better. Coach Bryant also had kind words for me afterward, telling reporters, "I don't know if the run by Nathan built a fire under our players, but I know it excited me."

We played at Washington the next week, and our trip to Seattle was the farthest I'd ever been from home. It took us forever to get there. That was a heck of a schedule Coach Bryant set up for us, and the trip to Washington might have been the most difficult road game. We had a hard time with the Huskies, but won 20–17 after Jeff threw a 36-yard touchdown to tight end Ricky Neal in the fourth quarter. Washington tried to come back in the final minutes, but our safety Murray Legg recovered a fumble with less than two minutes remaining to seal the victory.

Coach Bryant said, "I don't know if the run by Nathan built a fire under our players, but I know it excited me."

A lot of coaches say a team has to have luck to win a national championship. We certainly had our share of good fortune in 1978. Somehow, we beat Florida 23–12 on the road, overcoming six fumbles and nine penalties to win. We played much better at Tennessee the next week, though, and rolled to a 30–17 victory. The Tennessee game was always the biggest game of the season for Ken Donahue, one of our assistant coaches, and Jim Goostree, our trainer. Coach Donahue had played football for the Volunteers, and Goose was from Clarksville, Tennessee. Although the Iron Bowl against Auburn is the most important game for Alabama every season, the Tennessee rivalry runs pretty deep as well. Goose and Donahue liked to climb on equipment trunks in our locker room and tell us how important beating the Volunteers was to them. I'm glad we never let them down in our four seasons at Alabama.

After reeling off four victories in a row, we climbed up the rankings to No. 3. Remember what I said about needing luck? Well, October 1978 proved to be a pretty crazy month in college football. On October 14, No. 2–ranked USC lost at Arizona State and No. 5 Michigan lost to Michigan State. A week later, No. 3 Arkansas fell to Texas. Our roller-coaster ride was only beginning, with one-third of the season remaining.

We walloped Virginia Tech 35–0 in our homecoming game at Bryant-Denny Stadium on October 28. We defeated Mississippi State 35–14 at Legion Field a week later. The Bulldogs passed for a school-record 456 yards against us, but they couldn't stop our ground game. Ogilvie and I each scored two touchdowns, and I finished with 145 yards on twelve carries. Our offensive line was starting to maul people up front. We'd had to replace three starters from the previous year, but by the time Jim Bunch and Dwight Stephenson and three new guys gelled, they were pretty much unstoppable.

You want to talk about luck? Consider what happened to

us on November 11, 1978. We hosted No. 10–ranked Louisiana State University at Legion Field, needing a victory to stay in the hunt for both a Southeastern Conference title and a potential national championship. We trailed the Tigers 7–0 in the first quarter, and then LSU's Chris Williams intercepted one of Jeff's passes and ran 79 yards the other way to score. It looked like we were going to be behind by a 14–0 score. But the Tigers were penalized for clipping on Williams's return, which negated his touchdown, and then our defense made a big stop. Everything seemed to turn our way after that. We had a 17–10 lead in the fourth quarter, and then Williams muffed a punt return. Ikner recovered the ball for us at LSU's two-yard line, leading to Jeff's one-yard touchdown pass to McNeal for a 24–10 lead. We ended up winning the game 31–10.

But beating LSU wasn't even the biggest thing that happened for us that day. Nebraska upset No. 1–ranked Oklahoma 17–14, beating the Sooners for the first time in seven years. Oklahoma's loss propelled undefeated Penn State to the top spot in the polls and us to No. 2. To earn a chance to play for a national championship—an opportunity that seemed to be lost after we fell to USC in September—we only had to defeat Auburn in the Iron Bowl. Now, I'm not sure why the games were scheduled the way they were during the 1978 season, but we had to wait three long weeks to play the Tigers.

Believe it or not, we also needed help from Auburn, our biggest rival, if we were going to have a chance to play for a national championship. Like us, Georgia was also undefeated in SEC play and still in contention for the league championship. If Georgia beat Auburn on the road two weeks before the Iron Bowl, the Bulldogs would earn at least a tie for the SEC title. If we tied Georgia atop the final SEC standings, it would earn us a trip to the Sugar Bowl to play Penn State. At the time, SEC rules specified that in the case of a tie for first place, the team that most recently played in the Sugar Bowl would be bypassed. Wouldn't you know it? We received the best possible outcome when Auburn hosted Georgia on November 19, 1978. They played to a 22–22 tie. Talk about kissing your sister! We certainly couldn't root for Auburn to win, but we didn't want Georgia to win, either. We got the best of both worlds that day.

When the Iron Bowl finally came, on December 2, 1978, we were more than ready to play. It was an emotional game for Jeff and me. We were playing our last regular season games in our hometown of Birmingham. We were playing in the stadium where we'd squared off in high school. We also had a chance to lead the Crimson Tide to an unprecedented sixth consecutive victory over Auburn. Most important, we had to defeat the Tigers to earn a date against Penn State in New Orleans, where a national championship would be on the line.

Fortunately, Jeff played one of the best games of his college career, leading us to a 34–16 victory. He completed 13 of 21 passes for 174 yards with three touchdowns. He set an Alabama record with 30 career touchdowns, breaking the previous mark set by Joe Namath. After coming from behind to take a 17–13 lead at the half, we dominated the second half. It felt so sweet defeating Auburn four straight times in my career. Being young, I wanted to gloat and rub it in to every Auburn fan, and I knew plenty of them. But I had to hold it in and be a bigger man. I had to settle for having a big smile on my face every time I saw a Tigers fan. Once I was in the NFL, I enjoyed that guys like Joe Cribbs, William Andrews, and James Brooks (who were great running backs at Auburn) would see me and remember their defeat. But I didn't have to say anything to make them feel bad—not a word.

> Jeff Rutledge set an Alabama record with 30 career touchdowns, breaking the previous mark set by Joe Namath.

Of course, we still had one game left to play—a big one. It was hard to believe we were so close to fulfilling our dreams.

We felt pressure to win a national championship going into that final season. High expectations always existed at Alabama, but we faced even more pressure in 1978 because we'd come so close the year before but didn't get it done. When my recruiting class arrived at Alabama, the big emphasis was on winning bowl games, because previous teams struggled in the postseason. We took care of that problem by winning three bowl games in a row. Now, we wanted to end our college careers with the ultimate accomplishment, which was winning a national title.

During the month before the Sugar Bowl, we worked hard at practice to improve. We knew we'd have to be a well-oiled machine to beat the Nittany Lions, who had a 19-game winning streak and finished the regular season with an 11–0 record. Penn State was very good. They started the season ranked No. 3 and beat a handful of nationally ranked opponents, including No. 6 Ohio State, No. 5 Maryland, and No. 15 Pittsburgh. Nittany Lions running back Matt Suhey was a punishing runner. He would later become Walter Payton's lead blocker with the NFL's Chicago Bears. Penn State's quarterback Chuck Fusina was named All-American, along with offensive tackle Keith Dorney and defensive tackle Bruce Clark. Even their kicker Matt Bahr was named All-American. There was no doubt Penn State was going to be the best team we'd faced that season.

The Sugar Bowl, which was played on January 1, 1979, ended

up being one of the hardest-hitting games I ever played in. We knew it wasn't going to be a track meet. Playing the top-ranked team in the country, we were going to have to slug it out with the Nittany Lions. If Penn State hit us, we had to hit back twice. That's the kind of game it was going to be.

··

When you play in a game like the Sugar Bowl with so much at stake, you forget about conditions and what hurts and simply run.

··

Predictably, it was a defensive struggle for most of the first half. I had to fight for every yard I gained, and so did every other player on the field. On one of my early runs in the game, Bruce Clark and Matt Millen hit me at the same time. They hit me so hard I suffered a hip pointer. Those guys could really hit. Besides worrying about Penn State's defense, I was also concerned about the playing field inside the Superdome. AstroTurf may have been effective for playing in the rain, but it wasn't very good for players. It felt like concrete. Legion Field had the same kind of playing field, and I'd spend a week in the training room after playing games there. The trainers had to clean my wounds every day, and I couldn't even pull a sock over them. But when you play in a game like the Sugar Bowl with so much at stake, you forget about conditions and what hurts and simply run.

In my last college game, I wanted to make a play to help my team win. I so much wanted to win Coach Bryant another national championship. I also wanted one for my teammates. Finally, with about one minute left in the half, I broke loose in open field and ran to Penn State's 30-yard line. On the next play, Jeff threw a 30-yard touchdown to Bruce Bolton to give us a 7–0 lead. Honestly, we probably caught a big break on the play. Bolton caught Jeff's pass in the end zone and rolled to the ground. The pass looked incomplete, but the officials ruled it a touchdown. Thank goodness that game was played before instant replay. I'm not sure the play wouldn't have been overruled.

Late in the third quarter, Penn State tied the game at 7–7 on Fusina's 17-yard touchdown to Scott Fitzkee. It looked like the game was going to go down to the wire. But then Ikner, who was probably the fastest player on our team, returned a punt 62 yards to the Penn State 11. Three plays later, Ogilvie ran for an 8-yard touchdown to give us a 14–7 lead.

We knew Penn State wasn't going to quit. Late in the fourth quarter, Millen made a big play, forcing a fumble the Nittany Lions recovered at our 19-yard line with fewer than eight minutes to go. On the next play, Suhey ran for 11 yards for a first down at our eight-yard line. From the sideline, it looked like they were going to tie the score. But in what would become one of the greatest goal-line stands in college football history, our defense stopped Penn State on four straight plays, including the last two from our one-yard line. I'd never seen anything like it.

On first-and-goal from the eight-yard line, Mike Guman gained two yards on a toss sweep. On second down, Fusina dropped back and fired a pass to Fitzkee, who was slammed out-of-bounds by McNeal shortly before reaching the goal line. You can look long and hard, but you won't find a more textbook tackle than what McNeal made on the play. On third down, Suhey tried to dive over the top for a touchdown, but linebacker Rich Wingo tackled him short of the goal line.

I'll never forget what Marty Lyons told Fusnia before the famous fourth-down play. When Fusina came out to see how far the Nittany Lions were from the goal line during a timeout, he looked at Marty and asked, "How much is it?"

"'Bout this much,'" Marty said, while holding his hands close together.

"Ten inches?" Fusina asked.

"Yeah," Marty said. "You better pass."

On fourth down, however, Guman tried to run up the middle again. Our linebacker Barry Krauss came out of nowhere to stuff him for no gain. It's one of the most famous plays in Alabama football history. When Krauss made the tackle, I was sitting on the bench getting ready to go back in because there were still about five minutes left. After driving the ball away from our end zone, we caught another big break when Penn State had too many men on the field during a punt. The mistake gave us a first down, and then we kept the ball until there was about a minute left. We won the game by a 14–7 score.

Walking off the field in the Superdome, I knew we were going to be national champions. I knew the voters couldn't keep us from winning it again. It was icing on the cake for my college career. The next day, the Associated Press declared us national champions, while the United Press International coaches' poll declared USC its national champion. The Trojans beat us during the regular season and then defeated Michigan 17–10 in the Rose Bowl. I thought we were more deserving after beating the No. 1–ranked team in our bowl game—it's how Notre Dame won a national title the previous season—but I didn't mind sharing a championship.

After I left Alabama for the NFL, I was proud to watch many of my former teammates repeat as national champions the next season. The Crimson Tide went 12–0 in 1979 and won Coach Bryant his sixth national title, which is the most won by any coach in major college football history. Coach Bryant spent three more years on Alabama's sideline until retiring after the 1982 season. The Crimson Tide defeated Illinois 21–15 in the

Liberty Bowl in his final game. On January 25, 1983, Coach Bryant checked into a hospital in Tuscaloosa with chest pains. The next day, he suffered a massive heart attack and died. He was sixty-nine years old. When I learned of Coach Bryant's death, I couldn't believe he was gone.

Playing for somebody like Bear Bryant was a chance in a lifetime for me. The thing that made him a great coach was that he took the time to really get to know his players. I never saw the man greet one of his players without calling him by his name. Coach Bryant cared about you, and he was a father away from home for the whole team. There will never be another coach like him.

CHAPTER TWELVE

NFL

When I left the University of Alabama after the 1978 season, I was told I was probably going to be selected late in the first round of the 1979 NFL draft. If I didn't go in the first round, according to my agent, I was definitely going to be picked in the second. It didn't work out that way.

I can still remember watching the NFL draft with Johnnie, who was about to become my wife. We watched the draft in my apartment in Tuscaloosa, along with my parents and a few close friends. The NFL draft took place in New York on May 3–4, 1979. Back then the NFL didn't invite college players to the draft like they do today. The draft was televised, but it didn't have the wall-to-wall coverage we have now. Basically, I sat in my apartment and waited for my telephone to ring. Unfortunately, I waited and waited and waited.

Two of my Alabama teammates, linebacker Barry Krauss and defensive end Marty Lyons, were selected in the first round. Barry was the sixth pick overall by the Baltimore Colts, and Marty was the 14th pick by the New York Jets. After the first round ended without my name being called, Barry and Marty decided they were going to play a joke on me. They started calling my apartment, saying, "This is so-and-so from the Chicago Bears or the Washington Redskins. We've taken you with the thirty-ninth pick in the draft." That joke got old quickly. I was sitting there waiting for my phone to ring, and those knuckleheads didn't have anything better to do than to play a practical joke on me. There were 12 rounds in the 1979 NFL draft, and only the first two rounds were conducted on the first day. My name wasn't called on the first day, which made for a pretty sleepless night.

Finally, near the beginning of the third round on the second day, my telephone rang. The guy on the other end said, "This is

Chuck Connor from the Miami Dolphins." I said, "Yeah, right." I figured it was Barry or Marty calling me again. But then I heard a bunch of guys laughing in the background. It really was Chuck Connor, the director of player personnel for the Dolphins, and he had me on speakerphone with the team's coaches and scouts. Then I heard another man's voice.

> The guy on the other end said, "This is Chuck Connor from the Miami Dolphins." I said, "Yeah, right."

"Tony, this is Don Shula," he said. "What's the problem?"

"Get out of here," I said.

After a few seconds, Shula convinced me it really was him. The Dolphins selected me with the fifth pick of the third round, sixty-first overall. After sitting through the previous night, I was glad I didn't have to wait all day again. It was a long night waiting for my name to be called. After I was finally selected, I prayed and asked, "Lord, why did you put me through that?" But, you know, it's not about me. You might think the Lord is late, but He will always be on time for you. I have realized that many times over the years. His presence may not be evident when you want Him to be there, but then you figure out that He's been there all along, and His timing is always right. The Lord may have been humbling me that night and helping me appreciate the opportunity more. Maybe I was becoming a little too arrogant and starting to get a big head after a good college career. Maybe the Good Lord felt like I needed a little humbling. In the Bible, Matthew 23:12 teaches us: "For those who exalt themselves will be humbled, and those who humble themselves will be exalted."

There were nine running backs picked ahead of me in the 1979 NFL draft, including five in the first round. Some of those guys ended up having great NFL careers, while others didn't play for long. I wasn't exactly sure why I'd slipped in the draft. I had suffered a hip pointer against Penn State in the '79 Sugar Bowl, which caused me to run slower at my pro day in front of NFL scouts. I heard a couple of scouts say, "I thought the Nathan kid was faster," and I'm sure news of my injury made its way to other teams. The NFL draft has always been an inexact science and a crapshoot. Look at the guy who was the last pick of the third round in 1979—Notre Dame quarterback Joe Montana. He won four Super Bowl titles with the San Francisco 49ers and was inducted into the Pro Football Hall of Fame. There are plenty of guys who are overlooked or slip through the cracks in the NFL draft every year. When it happens, you have to believe in yourself and play hard, so you can show teams they were wrong about you. That's what I was determined to do.

I like to joke with my mother that she should have waited several years to have her firstborn son. If she and my father had waited a decade or two, I would have made a lot more money playing in the NFL. Back then, we didn't receive multimillion-dollar contracts like the players today. My first contract with the Dolphins included a signing bonus of $36,000. Barry and Marty received signing bonuses of more than $100,000 as first-round picks. I was happy for them, but I wasn't happy for me. My salary with the Dolphins was $36,000 the first year, $46,000 in the second, and $56,000 in the third. I remember telling Pops what I was going to make and he shook his head and started laughing. He was making $75,000 a year working at the steel mill. "You're supposed to be playing professional what?" he asked me.

Don't get me wrong: the bottom line is that I was happy to get drafted and have a chance to play in the NFL. God gave me a wonderful opportunity that not many people get, and it was up to me to make the best of it. I had to show the Dolphins' coaches what I could do and not leave it in their hands. Shula loved to draft Alabama guys. He knew the guys who played for Bear Bryant were going to be fundamentally sound and would work extremely hard. Shula drafted former Alabama linebacker

Bob Baumhower in 1977, and then he picked cornerback Don McNeal and center Dwight Stephenson in 1980. We were able to play together in Miami, which helped make my transition to the NFL much easier.

About six weeks after the Dolphins drafted me, Johnnie and I were married at New Bethel Baptist Church in Birmingham. My father was my best man; her sister Toni Wilson was the maid of honor. I'd proposed to Johnnie about a year earlier at my parents' house. I'm pretty sure I surprised her by asking her to marry me. We dated for eight years before we were married.

....

I became more cautious about what I was doing
and whom I was doing it with. I knew I had
to set a good example for my daughters.

....

My perspective in life totally changed when we had our first child. Nichole was born in 1980, Natalie came along in 1983, and then Nadia was born in 1987. After they came into our lives, raising a family with Johnnie became my priority. Football was still football; and I loved playing the game, and it was how I earned a living. But now other people were counting on me, and I knew I needed to be at home for my wife and daughters, as much as possible. When I wasn't at work, I knew I had to be with them and be serious about caring for my family. I became more cautious about what I was doing and whom I was doing it with. I knew I had to set a good example for my daughters. My father was the same way. He told us how things should be done and set an example for us. He told us, "If you talk the talk, you have to walk the walk." I still hung out with the guys sometimes, but I was very mindful that I was a parent.

I had no problem starting over, so to speak, when I went to the NFL. I had to learn the system and the NFL way of doing business. The veteran players liked to do different "initiation" things to the rookies, like taping us to a tree. I was taped to a tree. They made us sing our school fight songs. I found my helmet with grease and talcum powder in it one time. If you weren't paying attention, you'd put your helmet on and your face would be covered in grease and talcum powder. Another time, I found my jockstrap with balm in it—the hot stuff they put on sore muscles. Boy, that wouldn't have been much fun if I hadn't seen it. I also found water in my shoes. This was our initiation into the NFL. If you handled it, you gained respect from the veteran players.

Honestly, I think being initiated into the "A Club" at Alabama was worse than being initiated by the veteran players in Miami. It was a lot worse in Tuscaloosa. The upperclassmen at Alabama put you in a pair of overalls, with no shirt and no undershorts. They'd make the freshmen run around our dorm with eggs in our mouths. They'd tell us, "You better not break the yolks!"

Of course, I dealt with a different set of characters in Miami. There might have been maybe one or two conservative, faith-based guys in the Miami locker room. The majority were chain-smokers and dippers. It was buck wild in the locker room. Some of the veterans used to run faster when they were coming off the field than they did on it, heading for their cigarettes. It was the wildest thing I'd ever seen. I'd walk into our locker room and everybody was smoking—coaches and players. I was like, "Wow, this is different." Our coaches smoked at Alabama, but they didn't do it around us in the locker room. There were other wild things that happened in Miami. But I can't kiss-and-tell on my teammates. Even after all these years, I can't do it. Several single guys went out partying at night and, well . . . we'll leave it at that.

Anything can be intimidating at first because of the newness and uncertainty. But I was confident in my abilities and worked hard to prove to the Miami coaches that I could do the job. I had a good rookie season in 1979. My only goal that season was to get on the field, because I had been told that Shula didn't play many rookies. The first time I got into a game on offense, I was standing next to Shula on the sideline. It was third down, and our quarterback Bob Griese started pointing at me. He wanted me on the field with him. Shula looked at me, and then he looked back at Griese.

"Him?" Shula asked. "Uh-uh. Not him."

"Yeah, him," Griese said.

Thank goodness for Griese, or I probably wouldn't have been on the field very much as a rookie. Griese liked to have me on the field as a third-down back because I could catch the ball out of the backfield, which I didn't do much at Alabama. Griese was a smart quarterback and called his own plays. He ran the offense, and I thank God for that. That cat liked me, which was a good thing.

I also spent a lot of time during my rookie season doing extra practice with running back Delvin Williams and Nat Moore, one of our receivers. They stayed with me after practice and taught me how to become a better receiver. I knew I could catch the ball, but they showed me how to get off the line of scrimmage and properly run routes.

I arrived in Miami at the tail end of the Dolphins' dynasty. The 1972 Dolphins were the last NFL team to finish a season with an unbeaten record. They went 14–0 and no other NFL team has been perfect since. I was able to play with legendary players like Griese, Larry Little, Bob Kuechenberg, Larry Csonka, and Ed Newman. Csonka was still a beast in his final season in '79. People ran away from him so they wouldn't have to tackle him or fight through his blocks. The Dolphins were in a bit of a transition mode when I got there, bringing in younger guys to replace the veterans who were nearing the end of their careers. I realized pretty quickly that I was going to have to earn my way on the field.

Having to block guys who were a lot bigger and stronger than me was one of my biggest adjustments in the NFL. It was brute strength versus brute strength. The majority of those guys were much bigger than I was. I realized I had to play smarter, not harder. In practice, blocking drills were a nightmare. There was a one-on-one drill between linebackers and running backs. The coaches put a tackling dummy on the edge, and the linebacker would come around the horn, and you had to step up and put your screws in his chin. It was like street fighting. Of course, the linebacker had an advantage because he was running from ten yards back and had a flying start. I didn't. He could dip his head, bull rush you, get his hands to you, shake you, or try to beat you however he wanted. I had to find a way to block him, and I hated the drill.

Coach Shula was like Coach Bryant in that he made us work. We worked hard, sometimes practicing three times a day when we went to training camp. It was full pads in the morning, full pads after lunch, and then helmets and shoulder pads in the evening. I had to get used to practicing in the heat and especially the humidity and to wearing my pads when they were soaked wet from the rain. We practiced through quite a few South Florida pop-up showers. Mother Nature had very little mercy for us.

During my rookie season with the Dolphins, I mostly played on special teams. I was our team's primary kick returner. I had a good season and helped the team as much as I could. I averaged 22.6 yards on kickoff returns and 10.9 yards on punt returns. I didn't run the ball very often, but I was proving to be a pretty capable receiver out of the backfield. After the season, I was named an alternate for the Pro Bowl as a kick returner, which was a big honor for a rookie. It would have been fun to play in the game in Hawaii, but Billy "White Shoes" Johnson ended up going instead.

During my second season in 1980, I played a bigger role on offense. Delvin was our starting tailback and a good player. As the season progressed, I got more and more playing time. I had to overcome a big issue during those first couple of NFL seasons—fumbling. In '79, I fumbled the ball eight times. The next season, I fumbled nine times. I was taking more risks than I needed to, as I fought for extra yards. Coach Shula used to cuss me from A to Z for losing the ball. I understood why he did it, because I was giving up the rock, which was a valuable commodity. I had to learn to take care of the ball, or fumbles would be my ticket out of town. I started carrying a ball with me wherever I went—to the grocery store, the gas station, and to team meetings. Holding the ball became second nature to me. Coach Shula never took me off the field, and I loved him for having faith in me. I guess he saw something in me and thought I could help the team win, despite how many times I dropped the ball. After fumbling 17 times in my first two seasons, I fumbled only 17 times in the next seven seasons.

....

I had to learn to take care of the ball, or
fumbles would be my ticket out of town.

....

The 1982 season was a strange time for me. We opened the season by beating the New York Jets 45–28 and the Baltimore Colts 24–20. Then we didn't play another game for nearly two months because of a fifty-seven-day players' strike. Going on strike was something NFL players needed to do, not something we wanted to do. We had to make the game better for us. We needed better compensation, insurance, and more security after retirement. You don't want to bite the hand that feeds you, but it was time for the owners to take better care of us. We were being paid considerably less than professional baseball and basketball players, even though we were playing a much more violent sport. The NFL had signed a new five-year television contract that paid the owners more than two billion dollars. There wasn't even a free agency system in the NFL, and we weren't getting a fair share of the pie.

I wasn't a millionaire simply because I played in the NFL. Going on strike wasn't easy for me or my family. But I knew I had to stand with my fellow players. My father used to tell me, "If a man doesn't stand for something, he will fall for anything." I was willing to take a stand against the owners, but it certainly wasn't easy not getting paychecks. While we were on strike, I struggled to pay for our house, feed my family, and put gas in our cars. Somehow, the Good Lord made a way. I was fairly smart with my money. I didn't blow it. When I started hearing that we might go on strike, I watched our money even more carefully. During my first few seasons in the NFL, I actually sold cars during the off-season. Johnnie and I would take the girls back to Birmingham, where I worked at a Toyota dealership to make extra money. We'd rent our house in Miami for three months at a time and put our furniture in storage. We did this for three years. I still hate moving furniture today.

Once a new deal was reached between the players' union and team owners, the NFL tried to salvage the '82 season with a nine-game regular season. Because the season was shortened, the NFL decided to have a 16-team playoff, instead of a traditional eight-team format. We finished the regular season with a

7–2 record and made the playoffs. Then we got hot at the right time during the playoffs. We beat the New England Patriots 28–13 in the wildcard round and the San Diego Chargers 34–13 in the divisional round. Then we defeated the New York Jets 14–0 in the AFC Championship Game to earn a trip to Super Bowl XVII.

....

Coach Bryant died only four weeks
after coaching his final game.

....

I'll never forget Super Bowl XVII, for a couple of reasons. On January 26, 1983—four days before we played the Washington Redskins at the Rose Bowl in Pasadena, California—I was getting ready to board a bus to go to practice. It was at this time that I learned that Coach Bryant had died of a heart attack. I was shocked. I remember thinking about how my grandfather died shortly after he was forced to stop farming. Coach Bryant died only four weeks after coaching his final game. When you take something away that somebody loves, it hurts. It's like taking away their heart. I didn't get to attend Coach Bryant's funeral because of the Super Bowl, but I was with Baumhower, McNeal, and Stephenson when we found out he'd died. We shared quite a few stories about Coach Bryant that week.

Obviously, playing in my first Super Bowl was quite a thrill. We played well in the first half. In the first quarter, our quarterback David Woodley threw a 76-yard touchdown to Jimmy Cefalo to give us a 7–0 lead. After the Redskins tied the game at 10–10, Fulton Walker returned a kickoff 98 yards for a touchdown, the longest return in Super Bowl history. But after we took a 17–10 lead at the half, we couldn't slow down Washington's offense in the second half. The Redskins ran the ball down our throats—fullback John Riggins ran 166 yards on 38 carries for a Super Bowl record—and we couldn't get the ball back on offense. We ended up losing the game 27–17. It was a disappointing end to a terrific season.

The next spring, the Dolphins drafted quarterback Dan Marino in the first round of the 1983 NFL draft, and everything about our offense changed. The first time I saw Marino in practice, I knew there weren't many guys who could throw the ball like he did. Shula didn't start Marino from day one, but Dan took over in the sixth game of his rookie season in 1983. We became a completely different offense. He was elected to the Pro Bowl as a rookie and led us to a 12–4 record in the regular season. The next season, Marino became the first quarterback in NFL history to throw for more than 5,000 yards. He guided us to a 14–2 record during the 1984 regular season. We beat the Seattle Seahawks 31–10 in the divisional playoffs and the Pittsburgh Steelers 45–28 in the AFC Championship Game.

We were going back to the Super Bowl to play the San Francisco 49ers.

The buildup to Super Bowl XIX was all about the quarterbacks: Marino versus Montana. They were two of the most prolific passers in NFL history. The quarterback battle lived up to the hype during the first quarter. Marino completed nine of ten passes in the quarter, including a two-yard touchdown to Dan Johnson. Unfortunately for us, Montana was just as good. He ended up throwing for 331 yards with three touchdowns, while running for 59 yards with one score, and he led the 49ers to a 38–16 victory. We threw 50 passes in the game, and I caught ten of them for 83 yards. That was our game plan—ride Marino. The 49ers were very balanced on offense, and we just couldn't stop them. They gained 537 yards and their 38 points tied a Super Bowl record. Montana became the third player to be named a two-time winner of the Super Bowl MVP.

We had another good season in 1985, finishing the regular season with a 12–4 record. We beat the Cleveland Browns 24–21 in the divisional playoffs, but then lost to the New England Patriots 31–14 in the AFC Championship Game. I never got close to playing in the Super Bowl again. For whatever reason, we struggled mightily the next two seasons. We finished 8–8 in 1986 and 8–7 in 1987, which was another strike-shortened season. We missed the playoffs in both seasons.

I may have contributed to the Dolphins getting to two Super Bowl games, but that didn't help me after nine years with the team. The Dolphins cut me before my tenth season. Coach Shula and the other team executives told me there was a youth movement, and the team needed new blood. Nat Moore and I got the phone call on a Sunday morning after the 1987 season. Nat went into Coach Shula's office before me. He walked out of Shula's office and said, "They got me." I figured that's why I was there, too. Sure enough, Shula told me, "I hate to be the bearer of bad news. But I have to let you go." After talking with Coach Shula for a few minutes, he said, "Good luck. I hope you catch on with somebody else."

At the age of thirty-one, I thought my legs were still young enough to play a few more seasons in the NFL. I certainly didn't think my pro football career was over. In '85, I'd averaged 8.9 yards per carry and caught 72 passes out of the backfield. I still had plenty left in the tank as far as I was concerned. I knew I could still make my legs go. I thought that, surely, some other NFL team would pick me up. But when my agent contacted other teams, the executives told him, "We have to wait and see what Don Shula is going to do." I didn't know what they were waiting to see Coach Shula do or not do—he'd just called me into his office and cut me from the team. But I found out soon enough.

Shula brought me back to the Dolphins, but as an assistant coach. I asked him about the other teams not giving me a chance to play, and he laughed. It was an ego thing for him. He loved power and the fact that other people respected his wishes of not signing me before they checked with him. Hey, if you have that kind of clout, you have that kind of clout. I can respect that. The thing that hurt my chances of playing again was that the Dolphins still had me under contract, so they were using me as leverage for higher draft choices or money in a trade. That's why nobody touched me.

....

I was more like the assistants' assistant—I did whatever the assistant coaches didn't want to do.

....

Don't get me wrong: I was happy to still be working in professional football. I was blessed to have an opportunity to get into coaching after my playing career ended. I became Coach Shula's workhorse. At first, I wasn't actually an on-field assistant coach. I was more like the assistants' assistant. I did a lot of film study and advance scouting, along with whatever else the assistant coaches didn't want to do. The only thing they had to do was drop the work on my desk. But overall, it was a great learning experience, and I appreciated the opportunity.

I was fortunate to play professional football, and I'm certainly not disappointed with my career as a player or how it ended. Sure, I didn't get to put the icing on the cake with a Super Bowl victory, but I enjoyed every moment of my playing career. I got to play for great coaches and had great teammates, many of whom are still my closest friends. We won a couple of AFC championships, but I'd wanted to win a big ring with my team-mates. God truly blessed my life with sports and professional football. I know one thing: The Miami Dolphins paid me to practice. I played the games for free.

....

CHAPTER THIRTEEN

COACHING

After retiring as a professional football player in 1987, I have to admit that I was taken aback by my first coaching job in the NFL. At times, it was drudgery and involved menial tasks. But I learned a valuable lesson from the experience: there is nothing wrong with learning from the ground up. Very few people begin their careers on the top floor. If you come face-to-face with a job that you think is beneath you, embrace it. Twenty years down the road, you will thank yourself for going through it.

When I started coaching with the Miami Dolphins in 1988, we didn't have the technology that NFL teams use today. We didn't have helmet cameras, iPads, and fancy computer software. We had only pen and paper. One of my duties during the first season was charting plays. I had to watch every play in practice and write it down. First-and-10. Second-and-10. Whatever. Then I'd go to the coaches' meeting, go through each play with them, and write down their observations. I had a pen with four different colors, and that's how I charted plays. We didn't punch the plays into a hip laptop or iPad. It wasn't a lot of fun, but it's how other people started in coaching, and it's how I started as well.

At first, Miami Dolphins coach Don Shula said he couldn't pay me to be his assistant.

At first, Miami Dolphins coach Don Shula said he couldn't pay me to be his assistant. I was like, "What?" Coach Shula told me I had to find out whether I liked coaching. I told him I couldn't do the job for free, so he paid me $10,000 the first year. My pay gradually increased, like my salary as a player. I made $385,000 during my last season as a coach with the San

Francisco 49ers. That's exactly what I made during my last season as a player. Times were changing, and I was making good money, but it wasn't nearly as much as what the players are getting paid to play professional football nowadays.

Starting as a coach's assistant not only prepared me for a career in coaching, but it helped me in life. When I eventually became an on-field NFL assistant, college coach, and high school coach, I was able to talk to my players about the value of starting from scratch, as well as the challenges of being the low man on the totem pole. The grunt work taught me how to maintain my focus on my long-term goals and persevere. There was no silver spoon for me in the NFL. Even though I'd played in the league and had a good career, I was forced to start from the bottom floor of coaching, just like every other coach who wanted to be in the business. When I became a full-time assistant, I discovered that the menial tasks I had to do in the beginning helped me perform under pressure. I'd learned the terminology by charting plays and knew the game of football from the inside out. I knew how to watch video and break down plays, formations, and schemes. I became a vampire coach in the film room, watching plays over and over while I was alone in the dark.

My time as Coach Shula's assistant was my internship into the NFL. Don't let anybody tell you that it's not valuable to learn from the ground up. You have to sweep the floors before you can run the floor. Learn to take out the garbage. There is a certain amount of glamour that comes with working in the NFL, but there is a lot of nitty-gritty that happens behind the scenes before Sunday's kickoff.

After my playing career ended, I thought I might go back to selling cars and not get into coaching. But I loved the game of football. I wasn't ready to walk away from it. The time commitment needed to become a coach was even more consuming than when I was a player. Shula was an old-school coach. On most days, we arrived at the offices at six in the morning and didn't go home until well after midnight. A lot of Dolphins assistant coaches had air mattresses in their offices or in the locker room. We'd spend hours in our offices watching film and working on plays. Then Coach Shula would emerge from his office; we'd think it was finally time to go home. Instead, he would have a new idea he'd dreamed up while working in his office, and he'd want us to work on it right then—so we'd have to stay at the office even longer. That's the way it was in the NFL. We spent all our time working on a game plan, and then our head coach would come up with something else. We had to adjust on the fly and not complain.

Even though Shula cut me from the Dolphins before I was ready to retire as a player, I loved the guy. He gave me an opportunity to do something after playing and taught me how to be a professional. He was a hard man to work for, and he was demanding; but his work ethic rubbed off on me. I coached with the Dolphins from 1988 to 1995. I was Coach Shula's assistant from 1989 to 1992, and then I became the team's running backs coach. We had a couple of good seasons, reaching the AFC Championship Game in 1992 and making the playoffs three other times, but we never matched the success I had when I was a player.

In the beginning, Coach Shula didn't trust me enough to be involved in the personnel meetings. He told me I was too close to some of our players, many of whom had been my teammates. Some of those guys were older veterans, and Shula was afraid they'd ask me about what the team was going to do when roster cuts came. Sure enough, I had guys on the team asking me about what Shula and the other coaches thought about them. Coach Shula knew the players were going to come to me, so he didn't let me in the meetings to shelter me from uncomfortable situations. Finally, when most of my old teammates were gone—except for quarterback Dan Marino, who wasn't going anywhere—Shula let me be involved in the meetings.

Shula was honest with his players and those who worked for him. He told you what he thought about you. Coach Bryant had been the same way. If Coach Bryant didn't like you, he would tell you. Coach Bryant told some of his players, "Son, you are welcome to finish your education here, but you will never play for me." I heard him say that to some of the guys he recruited. Coach Bryant gave the guy a scholarship and honored it, but once he found out the guy couldn't play, he told him he was never going to see the field. Shula was just like Coach Bryant— right to the point.

When I became an on-field assistant in 1992, I tried to draw on my experiences as a player to help my guys perform better. If I could help a guy stay in the NFL longer by being smarter, that's what I did. Most young players wanted to come to practice and go home, so I had to teach them that that attitude wouldn't get them very far in the NFL. They needed to see how plays developed and watch film to see how it's done correctly. They had to be able to dissect the plays and learn from other people. They had to see what other players were doing and understand what made a player good. A lot of guys you went up against in the NFL were better than you might have thought they were. You needed to be ready before you stepped on the field and got knocked upside the head.

During my first season as the Dolphins' running backs coach, I worked with Terry Kirby of Virginia, Keith Byars of Ohio State, and Mark Higgs of Kentucky. We also had Bernie Parmalee, who was actually a driver with UPS before we signed him. Byars wanted to be a fullback in our offense, but he was a tight end. He was a big man.

I loved coaching those kids. I had my share of troublemakers, but it was just a matter of time before they learned that I was going to outlast them if they kept screwing up. Mostly, they were good guys in the locker room and off the field. My running backs knew they had to show up on time for meetings—that was Shula's most important rule. If they weren't at a meeting on time, I wasn't covering for them. They knew I'd turn in their names for being late, which meant they were going to be fined. I didn't have a choice; it was my job or theirs. I wasn't going to lose my job over a kid being late. I was going to teach them the responsibility of being where they needed to be on time. I used to tell my players, "Don't meet me there—beat me there."

My coaching style was to make sure my guys knew exactly what they had to do on every play. I spent as much time as needed to make sure they understood what we were trying to do. There were no excuses on Sunday—none. Shula was the kind of coach who thought "more was better." He believed in that phrase. I had to spend extra time with my players and get them to understand their responsibilities on every play. Coach Shula liked to say that NFL plays work like a clock. If one tick is off, then a play is doomed. I spent as much time as possible with my players in the film room, talking about different schemes and different looks from defenses. Everyone learns differently. Guys were coming to our team after playing different schemes in college and they had to learn an entirely new system.

We mixed words and numbers in our terminology, and I had to get it straight in their heads. When somebody hears a number, nine times out of ten, they know the base play and what everyone is doing. Otherwise, the quarterback would go through pass routes in the huddle, and bedlam would break out around him on the field.

My coaching style was to make sure my guys knew exactly what they had to do on every play.

Some of my rookies had a deer-in-the-headlights look. I started working with them from day one, right from scratch, making sure they understood protection on a three-man front or four-man front. I had to teach them what to do if a defense gave us an eagle or a bear front with seven defenders in the box. If a defense loaded the box—the area within seven yards of the line of scrimmage—they had to know there were too many players to block. Somebody was going to be coming at our quarterback. The quarterback needed to know which side the defender was coming from because we couldn't block them all. Football is a complicated game.

One thing Shula didn't like was his Hall of Fame quarterback getting hit. Marino didn't like to get hit, either. If one of my guys couldn't block, he couldn't play. That's basically what it boiled down to. A guy might know what to do, but eventually the defender he has to block will be bigger or better or maybe just younger. If that guy didn't get the job done on a blocking assignment, Shula would find me in a heartbeat on the sideline. He would tell me, often in not-so-kind words, "If he can't get the job done, get him out and get somebody else in there." It was my responsibility to make sure Marino didn't get hit.

I coached with the Dolphins until Coach Shula retired after we went 9–7 in 1995. Team owner Wayne Huizenga wanted Coach Shula to shake up his coaching staff, but he refused to fire any of us. Instead, Coach Shula decided to walk away after a thirty-three-year career, in which he'd won more games than any other coach in NFL history. The other assistants and me were also out of jobs.

After Coach Shula retired, I coached running backs for the Tampa Bay Buccaneers under Tony Dungy from 1996 to 2001. He was an amazing coach and an even better man. He was a lot like Coach Bryant and Coach Shula. He was a man of faith and cared deeply about his players and the men who worked for him. Under Tony's leadership, we helped change the entire attitude of people in Tampa about the team. We became winners. After finishing 6–10 in our first season in 1996, we finished at least .500 or better in each of the next five seasons. From 1979 to 1995, the Buccaneers finished with a winning record only twice in a full season. We changed the uniforms, culture, and drafted a lot of good players during our time there. Even though we won a lot of football games in Tampa Bay, our coaching staff was fired after the 2001 season. The next season, the Buccaneers won Super Bowl XXXVII during coach Jon Gruden's first season. Tony took the head coaching job with the Indianapolis Colts, and decided to keep the running backs coach that was already there.

I coached a lot of special players in the NFL. Warrick Dunn, one of my running backs with the Buccaneers, was one of the best men I ever coached. On the field, Warrick did things as a rookie and on his own that we as coaches did not anticipate. He was football savvy and made his own adjustments on the fly. There were a few times when our offensive coordinator would say to me during a game, "Where is Warrick going?" Once we watched the film, however, we'd see that the guy Warrick was supposed to block on a pass protection went somewhere else, so Warrick adjusted and made a block on somebody else's man so we could get the ball off. Warrick could make an adjustment in a heartbeat.

Some people had concerns about Warrick's size; and I did, too, when I first started coaching him. He was about 5 feet, 10 inches tall. But I can tell you, he was more durable than most big backs. He definitely had a bigger heart and more determination. Warrick was sturdy and tough and could run between the tackles or outside. He would get defenses moving one direction and then he'd plant his foot and run back the other way. When he did it during games, I'd often hear a coach on the sideline say, "No, he can't cut back there," and then I'd say, "Oh, yes, he can."

Warrick was a great player and a great man. His mother, Betty Sommers, worked as a police officer in his hometown of Baton Rouge, Louisiana. On January 7, 1993, shortly before Warrick enrolled at Florida State University, armed robbers murdered his mother while she escorted a businesswoman to a bank to make a night deposit. Warrick's father wasn't in his life, so, along with his grandmother, he was left to help raise his younger brothers and sisters. Even while I coached Warrick in Tampa Bay, he would work as an NFL player during the day and then help his brothers and sisters do their homework at night. Each of his siblings became productive citizens; he did a great job helping to raise them.

While coaching in Tampa Bay, I also had a special relationship with fullback Mike Alstott. Mike was a hard worker and really smart. After the Buccaneers drafted Mike in 1996, his coaches at Purdue University told us he was as dangerous with the ball as he was without it. Mike knew how to block, but he could also run. Mike was 6 feet, 1 inch tall and weighed about 250 pounds. He had great feet for a big man. He could also see where a hole was opening and would always hit it at the right time. Mike wanted to be a tailback. In his heart, he wanted the ball, just like every other running back.

....

Warrick Dunn was a great player and a great man.

....

After the coaches were fired in Tampa, I went back to Miami and spent a year coaching at Hialeah-Miami Lakes High School. It was fun to get back to coaching kids. Then I took a job at Florida International University in 2003, working under Don Strock, one of my former Dolphins teammates. It was the first time in my coaching career that I had to recruit players. I used to ride around South Florida to visit players with my good friend Hurlie Brown, who was FIU's secondary coach. I also re-cruited the Panhandle area of Florida, so I put quite a few miles on my car. My job in recruiting was to identify kids who had fallen through the cracks and weren't being recruited by bigger schools. Some of them became decent players for FIU. I had to watch a lot of film to see if a player caught my eye. Did he show up for the game in a big way? What was he good at? I would look at his feet, his intensity, and whether he was dependable. And I had to determine whether he had the ability to compete against good competition.

I spent three seasons coaching at FIU, and then I went back to the NFL as a running backs coach with the Baltimore Ravens in 2006 and then the San Francisco 49ers in 2008. It was the life of a coach, always on the move. I know it wasn't easy on my family. Halfway through my one season with the Niners, the team fired Coach Mike Nolan and hired Mike Singletary to replace him. I was out of a job again.

I stayed in coaching for a few seasons, helping at American Heritage High School in Plantation, Florida, and Boca Raton High School in Boca Raton, Florida. It was different going back to high school football more than thirty years after I'd left Woodlawn High. When I was at Woodlawn, playing high school football was more of a team thing. Nowadays, players seem more concerned about their individual statistics and futures. In my opinion, it's too much about "me."

When I coached at the high school level, the kids on my teams kept saying "I." "I want to do this," or "I am best in such and such position." But I told them, "Hold on, brother, this is a football team. We're here to win football games as a team." Then I'd tell them about what Coach Bryant said to me about not having lightning bugs on his teams. I might as well have been speaking French to them. So many of the kids were playing only

217

for themselves, trying to earn a scholarship to college. I couldn't blame them; for a lot of them football might have been their only ticket to a college education. Most of their parents couldn't afford to send them to college. But kids need to understand that God is the one who gives us our talents. Maybe a father or coach can enhance a kid's talent, but you either have God-given talent or you don't. I knew I was blessed to play football at Alabama and in the NFL. The only reason I was able to reach those levels was because of the talents God had given me.

....

Kids need to understand that God is
the one who gives us our talents.

....

Lots of kids want to play football at a high level but don't have the ability. There are only a total of 85 scholarships available for each of the Football Bowl Subdivision college teams. So obviously, not everybody gets one. When I coached in high school, I had to tell players' parents that their sons' futures were not more important than the team as a whole. I was there to help each player maximize his talent. I wasn't there to put one player ahead of another.

Both players and parents needed to understand the system. Look at Jeff Rutledge. He had a terrific arm and was a great passer, but he came to play at Alabama and to be part of some-thing big—even though he knew that his position there would dictate that he'd run the ball much more than he'd throw. Jeff understood the system of playing football, and he was happy to do what worked for his team.

The worst year I had coaching was at Dade Christian School in Hialeah, Florida. My wife, Johnnie, was teaching there, and my daughters attended the school. I coached there for one year. If I told my players one thing in practice, their mothers and fa-thers would tell them something different at home. It was totally different from when I played for Tandy Gerelds at Woodlawn High School and Coach Bryant at Alabama. I actually had to tell parents they could tell their kids whatever they wanted at home, but when they walked inside the gate of the football field, those kids had to listen to me. And, above everything else, I had to ask the parents not to help me coach.

Despite the problems, I had fun coaching, especially after we worked all week in practice and then executed our game plans perfectly on Friday night. Maybe a player would finally believe in what I was telling him. Once the play worked, his eyes be-came filled with joy as he came off the field. I would say, "Hey, I appreciate you listening to me." And if he said, "Thank you," I felt great satisfaction. Those were the moments that kept me going in coaching.

Throughout my coaching career—whether it was for an

NFL team or high school rookies—I loved my players and tried to earn their trust. I took the approach that they were my guys. I quickly learned that your players will show you in training camp whether they can do the job. You just get a feeling about them. Very rarely are you going to find two running backs who have the same ability and the same intellect. Every player lacks something, and it's the coach's job to figure out what it is and not embarrass the kid because of it. You're going to need that kid one day. He needs to know you are on his side and that you want only the best for him. There have been times in my coaching career when the offensive coordinator and I fell out—just couldn't get along—because I protected the men I was coaching. I got into disagreements with head coaches or the offensive line coach because my guys were my guys. I looked out for them.

As a coach, I made it a point not to be over-the-top about playing for Coach Bryant and Coach Shula. I didn't tell my guys, "This is how I did it for Bear Bryant or Don Shula. This is the only way to do it." I was their coach; I wasn't some legendary figure like Bryant or Shula. I had to interact with my players in my own way. Of course I thought about how Coach Bryant and Coach Shula dealt with me and coached me, but I never said, "Hey, listen, Bear Bryant was my coach. I know what I'm doing." It would never have worked.

One of the many things I learned from Coach Bryant was to

respect each player enough to call him by his first name. Even if someone else had to walk up behind Coach Bryant and whisper the player's name in his ear, he always made the effort. Knowing a guy's name makes your relationship personal, and I think players trust you more as a result.

I always made it a point to know everybody in my meeting room. Some players would let you into their lives and others wouldn't. I didn't pry. Some players would come to me for advice or help, other players wouldn't. But once a player opened that door, I tried to find out everything I could about him. I'd find out what was weighing on his mind or what was keeping him from performing to his full potential. I found that if players were willing to confide in me, I had a much better chance of helping them. I brought them into my office and had sit-down meetings with them. Some players would take their problems from practice home, which was never good. Then the least little thing might set them off with their families. Some guys have the ability to separate work and home, but other guys find it more difficult.

I almost didn't get into coaching, but I'm certainly glad I did. I almost missed out on the satisfaction that comes from working with younger guys. I'll never forget the morning Coach Shula called me into his office and cut me from his team. I had to look in the mirror of my mind and say, "Nate, what are we going to do?" What was I going to do? I didn't finish school, and I didn't have my degree from the University of Alabama. I hadn't even thought about coaching. But I worked hard at coaching and made my way in the profession from the ground up. I learned to be a professional, studied my trade, and asked people for help when I needed it. More than anything else, I tried to make a positive impact on kids. Believe it or not, winning games was only a small part of it.

CHAPTER FOURTEEN

....

PRAISE YOUR POND

When I was growing up, my mother liked to tell me, "It's a poor frog that doesn't praise his own pond." What she was telling me is that it's okay to praise yourself for your own accomplishments, as long as you do it in a respectful and humble manner. As a football player, I believed in myself and had plenty of confidence. I knew I could get the job done when needed. I think I had a good career playing football. I praise my pond and the abilities that I was given by the Good Lord.

I also learned that when you see the good in yourself, it's much easier to see the good in others—and to praise them. I was blessed to play on great teams and be influenced by tremendous coaches at Woodlawn High School, the University of Alabama, and the Miami Dolphins. I also praise the people who crossed my path during my athletic career and the people I come across now after football. I continue to be grateful for my opportunities and how others have helped me. I have helped myself by working hard and being disciplined. I praise my own pond, but I know there are others around me who contributed greatly to my life.

Ed Newman is one of those men. He was a teammate while I was with the Dolphins, and he contributed greatly to my life. Ed grew up in New York and was a star football player at Duke University. He was also a two-time Atlantic Coast Conference heavyweight wrestling champion—the real kind of wrestling and not the fake stuff we see on TV. The Dolphins selected Ed in the sixth round of the 1973 NFL draft. He played 12 seasons with Miami and became one of the best guards in the NFL. Honestly, Ed was an overachiever as a player. He probably weighed only 250 pounds when he played. Miami coach Don Shula liked his offensive linemen to be light and quick. Ed was quick, but he was also exceptionally strong. He could bench-press more than 500 pounds, and defensive linemen had a difficult time moving him.

....

Ed Newman could bench-press more
than 500 pounds, and defensive linemen
had a difficult time moving him.

....

Over the years, I learned that Ed is as good a man as he is a football player. During the 1975 season, Ed beat thyroid cancer and continued to play football. He also overcame three serious knee injuries during his career. Ed is one of the toughest guys I know, but he also has an extremely big heart. He did so much charitable work during his time as a player that the city of Miami honored him by renaming Northwest 17th Street "Ed Newman Street."

I knew Ed was an intelligent man because he liked to ask so many questions during our team meetings. While the rest of us were ready to get out of there, Ed wanted to stay and learn as much as he could. In 1984, while still playing with the Dolphins, Ed started taking night classes at the University of Miami's School of Law. I can't imagine the discipline and stamina it required to go to practices and team meetings during the daytime and then go to law school classes and study at night. Ed graduated from law school in 1987, became a practicing attorney, and then was elected a county court judge in Miami in 1994.

> After Ed spent his playing career protecting
> guys like me on the football field, it was going
> to be my job to protect him in the courtroom.

After I retired from high school coaching, I attended a Dolphins game and saw Ed there. He said he'd heard I was looking for a job. I told him I was trying to get back into coaching in the NFL. Ed said, "I have a job for you right now." He wanted me to be his bailiff. I had no clue what a bailiff did in a courtroom, other than what I'd seen those guys do on TV shows like *Judge Judy* and *The People's Court*. Basically, after Ed spent his playing career protecting guys like me on the football field, it was going to be my job to protect him in the courtroom. I accepted the job and told him, "As long as I don't have to put my hands on anybody, I'll be good."

I've worked as Ed's bailiff in the Richard E. Gerstein Justice Building in Miami for the past six years. It's a good job, but I've learned that a courtroom can become heated and emotional. The people who are accused of crimes have to come to terms with their mistakes and there can be arguments. I carry pepper spray, just in case somebody gets a little too belligerent. The courtroom is like my house, and I want people to act right in my house. There's no yelling and no screaming in Ed's courtroom. I make sure everyone abides by the rules. If there is a problem, Ed wants me to let him know. Police officers are in the courtroom for trials, so there is help if I need it.

Ed is the type of judge who likes to give first-time offenders enough of a spank on the hand that they'll stop doing what they're doing wrong. If someone is a repeat offender, though, Ed will follow state guidelines and that's when there can be trouble. If a defendant comes back in front of Ed after he has shown him or her some leniency and asked them to clean up their behavior, chances are it isn't going to be pretty. If state guidelines dictate a thirty-day sentence, Ed might give the person twenty-five days. If it's someone's third offense, he'll often tell the defendant, "You don't want to learn." Then Ed lets the defendant spend time in the hotel that has bars for windows.

Ed is a great judge for troubled young people to come before. He's well-spoken and evenhanded. But he is cordial in the courtroom only to a point. Defendants can't come into his courtroom and talk back to him. If they do, he will have the situation under control quickly. We also follow a rule we learned from Coach Shula. We couldn't be late to practices or team meetings, and defendants can't be late to court.

The courtroom can also get ugly if an attorney tries something sneaky. If an attorney tries a legal tactic that Ed deems against the rules, well, Ed will have a problem with it. Ed has been around long enough to know that the right way is the right way. Slick attorneys aren't allowed to circumvent the legal process and maneuver around Ed. They better know the law, understand what is allowed, and not play games. I sit in amazement, sometimes, watching how Ed follows the law and handles cases. I don't know a lot about the law, but Ed explains it to me afterward. He understands how to deal with people and what needs to be done to keep the community safe.

Ed's court is a misdemeanor court, and he doesn't handle cases involving juveniles. But a lot of the defendants who come into his court are eighteen or nineteen years old. It's difficult for me to watch young people go through the criminal justice system. I try to talk to some of the younger kids. If I'm taking a kid to processing, I might say to him, "Why do you do this? What's wrong?" Some kids look at me and say, "Man, please, leave me alone." But there are a few kids who respond to me, and then I try to offer them advice and encourage them to try to do things differently. But if they don't listen and aren't willing to improve their situation—it's straight to jail they go.

I always try to plant a seed with the ones who are receptive. I don't try to be a preacher, but I can make a quick point to them about changing their lives and acting differently. More than anything, I try to convince them that they don't want to come back to Ed's courtroom as a repeat offender. I tell them there is a higher authority out there who can do things for them that no man on this earth can do. Kids need to have a pipeline to God when they feel as if they don't have anyone else.

....

> I tell them there is a higher authority
> out there who can do things for them
> that no man on this earth can do.

....

A lot of the kids who get into trouble try to say they were hanging with the wrong crowd or were simply in the wrong place at the wrong time. I tell them that it might be time for them to change their circle of friends. Like I said, I'm not a preacher, but I suggest that they might want to consult with a higher authority to change their lives.

Unfortunately, a lot of kids who come into Ed's courtroom don't have any direction. Many of them come from broken homes and don't have fathers in their lives. I think my role in Ed's courtroom is kind of like coaching. I see kids come through the court who have been charged with crimes like possession of marijuana or driving under the influence. I try to coach them to find a different path in their lives. I warn them that the little stuff can lead to bigger stuff, which will undoubtedly set them back in life.

I also encourage some of the kids to get involved in sports. Football and other sports keep kids out of trouble. Instead of walking around looking for mischief, kids have practices and games. Sports keep some of them busy. When I was a kid, I played three sports and was a part of traveling teams in basketball that kept me occupied. It was a lot of fun, not just something for me to do to stay out of trouble. Athletics were a major part of my life growing up, and I think kids today aren't being encouraged enough to participate in sports. They're spending too much time on the streets with too much free time on their hands.

I'm thankful that my parents did a tremendous job of steering me away from the trouble I see so many kids going through today. The wheels could have fallen off while I was growing up in Birmingham. There was temptation all around me. If I ran with the wrong crowd—kids who did what they wanted when they wanted—my parents put me in my place when I came home. I am thankful for that discipline. That kind of fear is respect. I feared my parents because I knew they would whip my butt for stepping out of line.

Parents should not shy away from disciplining their kids. Fortunately, my kids stayed out of trouble because Johnnie and

I were vigilant about things going on around their schools and our community. But I'll tell you one thing: when they did get into trouble, they didn't call their mother to get them out of hot water, because she was usually more stern than I was. Thankfully, my three daughters turned out to be good kids. My oldest, Nichole, attended the University of South Florida, and Natalie and Nadia both attended the University of Alabama on a Bryant Scholarship—which Coach Bryant established in '73 to help pay tuition costs for the sons and daughters of his former players. It doesn't matter if a player is an All American or a walk-on. If his child wants to attend Alabama, there is money available to help pay for educational costs. It's yet another example of how great a man Coach Bryant was and how much he cared for his players.

Even as I'm about to begin my sixth decade on this earth, I'm still learning and listening to what other people have to say. When I left Alabama for the NFL in 1979, I hadn't yet finished my college degree. After playing in the Sugar Bowl and then a few college all-star games after my senior season, I fell behind in my studies. When I returned to campus, a couple of my professors told me they didn't think I could catch up and advised me to drop the classes. I had to get Coach Bryant's permission to drop the courses, and he made me promise him I'd return to Alabama and finish my degree. I was only ten credits short of graduating from Alabama. Over the years, my wife, my daughters, and my brothers and sisters continued to pester me about finishing my degree requirements. When I walked down the hallway of our house, where my wife and daughters have their college diplomas hanging on the wall, one of them would sometimes say to me, "What's missing?"

Finally, I listened to my family. I hadn't been in a hurry to finish my college degree, but my wife and daughters really wanted me to earn it. So during the past couple of years, I completed my courses online and earned a bachelor's degree in general studies from the University of Alabama. I received my diploma in May 2015, nearly four decades after I first walked on the campus in Tuscaloosa. What can I say? My wife and daughters wore me down. I joke about it, but it's something I needed to do. It is an accomplishment, and I can honestly say that I praise my pond for finishing my degree.

I received my diploma in May 2015,
nearly four decades after I first walked
on the campus in Tuscaloosa.

When I look back on my football career, I think winning a national championship at Alabama was my biggest achievement.

We didn't win a state title at Woodlawn High School and didn't win either of the two Super Bowls I played in with the Dolphins. I didn't get a chance to put the icing on the cake with those two teams, which is a regret.

I never was the kind of player who focused on individual statistics. If I'd wanted a lot of individual attention, I guess I would have played an individual sport like golf or tennis. But I was more team-oriented, and my goals were related to the team and how we finished a season. I was happy with what I accomplished in terms of rushing yards and touchdowns, but I judged success by my teams' records and championships.

I think my personality was suited for team sports. I liked to see how a team came together and how collective work resulted in success. When everything came together on a Friday night, Saturday, or Sunday, I always thought winning a football game with the guys was a great achievement. And it was a lot of fun. We won a national championship at Alabama in 1978 because we were truly a team. We didn't have any superstars, and no one was more important than someone else. We shared the wealth. Coach Bryant made me believe I was only part of a team, and that was a great lesson for me and the other players he coached. That's probably one of the reasons Alabama didn't have a Heisman Trophy winner until running back Mark Ingram won the award in 2009. The Crimson Tide had many great players over the years, but Coach Bryant and the coaches who succeeded him always put more emphasis on the team than individuals. That's the culture at Alabama.

....

> I liked to see how a team came together and
> how collective work resulted in success.

....

I was truly blessed to have mentors who were special people. Men like Coach Bryant, Coach Shula, and Coach Gerelds played important roles in my life. It was a two-way street. I either made a choice to go along with the program, or I was going to be shipped out by those guys. The choice was simple: I was a part of their programs and their teams. When they saw that I was willing to work and listen, they gave me an opportunity to improve myself.

But I can't leave out Hank Erwin. That Monday afternoon as I sat alone on the bleachers, I was thinking about how I was ever going to be a worthwhile running back. Hank saw me and climbed the steps to sit beside me. I'll never forget what he said. "I have something I've wanted to say to you since the first time I saw you run," Hank began. "There's something special about you, Tony. It's something that can't be taught. It can only be given. And you have to decide what to do with it. Now, when you play for yourself, you can be great. But when you play for a purpose higher than yourself, well, that's when extraordinary things can happen."

It was that day that it all came together for me—what my parents had taught me, what I'd been learning from Coach Gerelds, and what I was learning on the field. It was then and there that I first had the vision of playing with a purpose. I wanted to play for the benefit of the whole team, but even more, I wanted to help bring our team together—black and white.

From that day forward, I turned my life over to the Lord and gave everything I had in practice to become the best player I could possibly be. Only God knew what was going to happen to me next. I had no idea then that the climactic game between Woodlawn and Banks would help bring the whole city of Birmingham together and begin the healing of a racially torn community.

And now, I must finish my story with where my life began— with my father. Pops was an amazing mentor and is my best friend. He was a lot like Coach Bryant, Coach Gerelds, and Coach Shula. He prepared me to play for those men by instilling discipline and respect in me. Pops continuously pushed me to do the right thing, to be on time, and to always put others above myself. I thank my father for teaching me those important lessons, which undoubtedly had an impact on my life.

Would Coach Gerelds have trusted me to handle a difficult

situation without the tolerance and respect for others my father taught me? Would Coach Bryant have recruited me without the discipline I learned from Pops? Would Coach Shula have drafted me, kept me on his teams for my entire NFL career, and then hired me as an assistant coach if I hadn't witnessed and learned from my father's work ethic? My life would have turned out very differently if Pops hadn't loved me enough to teach me those lessons.

....

> My life would have turned out very differently if Pops hadn't loved me enough to teach me those lessons.

....

More than anything, Pops taught me that to earn respect, a man first has to give respect. To have a friend, a man has to be a friend. I learned those valuable lessons by watching his example. He respected and loved people. My dad never met a stranger. He could talk it up with anyone, and I think that rubbed off on me. I was able to get along with my teammates and coaches, which is important both in football and in life. You want to have a good locker room, not a bunch of guys who don't like each other. Pops taught me how to love others.

I think the most important things I learned from my parents were to be humble and appreciate my God-given opportunities. If you can run fast or jump high, well, your abilities came from somewhere. Sure, you have to be confident in yourself. But we must also remember that our talents are on loan from God. It is up to us to develop those talents and to cherish them. I still thank God every day for what He has given me, and I thank Him for instilling in me the desire to run and live with a purpose.